Emily Dickinson
A Voice of War

Emily Dickinson
A Voice of War

Shira Wolosky

Yale University Press
New Haven and London

811
D553Ywo

Designed by Nancy Ovedovitz and set in ITC Zapf International type by The Composing Room of Michigan, Inc. Printed in the United States of America by Vail-Ballou Press, Binghamton, New York.

Library of Congress Cataloging in Publication Data
Wolosky, Shira, 1954–
    Emily Dickinson: a voice of war.
    Bibliography: p.   Includes index. 1. Dickinson, Emily, 1830–1886—Criticism and interpretation.   I. Title.
PS1541.Z5W6   1984   811'.4   83-27405
ISBN 0-300-03109-2

The paper in this book meets the guidelines for permanence and durability of the Committee on Production Guidelines for Book Longevity of the Council on Library Resources.

1   3   5   7   9   10   8   6   4   2

In Memory of
Dr. Gerald Wohlberg

1939–1973

And when Joshua heard the noise of the people as they shouted, he said unto Moses, there is a voice of war in the camp. And he said, it is not the voice of them that shout for mastery, neither is it the voice of them that cry for being overcome: but the noise of them that sing do I hear.

Exodus 32:17–18

Contents

With Gratitude—

To my teachers and my colleagues, for the encouragement, interest, and support they have unceasingly given to me and which have been truly extraordinary. With special thanks to Robert Fagles, for his enthusiasm, energy, and insight; to A. Walton Litz, for his continuous encouragement and generous advice; to Emory Elliott, Joseph Frank, and Ralph Freedman, for their time, their knowledge, and their wonderful encouragement. And to those who have read the manuscript of this book and have helped with it: to John Hollander, for his scrupulous reading of the manuscript and his many suggestions for its improvement; to Harold Bloom, for his suggestions, warmth, and insight; to Leslie Brisman, for his careful and daring suggestions on the readings of poems; to Jaroslav Pelikan, for his invaluable discussions of theology and guidance on bibliography; to Alan Trachtenberg, for his generous advice and interest. And to all those who have read chapters, offered advice, made suggestions, and given encouragement, I give my heartfelt thanks.

To my friends, from whom I have learned as I have learned from my teachers. With special thanks to Gail Berkeley and Beverly Haviland, whose ideas have deeply influenced my own and who have sustained me more than they can imagine; to Rickey Wolosky, for reasons too great and too many to be recounted; to Susanne Wofford, for her joy in discussing ideas; and to Susan Israel, for long years of friendship.

To Little, Brown & Company, the Harvard University Press, and Houghton Mifflin Company for their permission to cite Dickinson's poetry.

To the Whiting Foundation, the Fulbright-Hayes/Israel Government Grant Program, and the American Council of Learned Societies for their generous fellowship support.

To my family—my father, my mother, my sisters and brother—who are an unending source of love and strength; to my new family, in all their generations. Above all, to my parents, who have been my most sustaining fellowship. And to my husband, with all my heart.

S. W.

Introduction

For all men who say yes, lie.

—Herman Melville, *Letters*

Emily Dickinson's poetry has rarely been approached in terms other than the private and personal. Even when wider contexts to her work have been admitted, they continue to be defined by her presumably self-enclosed and eccentric sensibility. That sensibility is further portrayed—by biographers, critics, and anthologists—as one of shy, frail timidity. Frightened by the world and disappointed in her hopes, Dickinson, it is said, retreated into a privacy that shielded her from exterior involvement. There, in accordance with the particular interpretation adopted, she is established as a martyr: to a lost love, to a neurotic state, to a religious ideal, or to her own literary pursuits. But Dickinson's verse, contrary to traditional conceptions of it, registers issues and events outside of her private sphere. Her poetry, when approached without the assumption of her complete isolation, can be seen as profoundly engaged in problems of the external world and aggressively so. It presents a point of intersection of literary, cultural, and metaphysical concerns, an arena in which conceptual structures and historical pressures implicate and generate linguistic configuration.

Privacy and fear are certainly present in Dickinson's work, as are anguish and morbid sensitivity. But their quality is different from that generally presumed. The overwhelming effect of Dickinson's verse is not delicacy. It is ferocity. Dickinson is an assertive and determined poet, as much fury as maiden, whose retirement is a stance of attack, whose timidity is aggressive. Her poetry leaves an impression of defiance rather than detachment, and her poetic is neither helpless nor quaking. It is, rather, one of ironic twists, sudden stabs, and poison:

> Go slow, my soul, to feed thyself
> Upon his rare approach—
> Go rapid, lest Competing Death
> Prevail upon the Coach—
> Go timid, should his final eye
> Determine thee amiss—
> Go boldly—for thou paid'st his price
> Redemption—for a Kiss-[1]

This poem, never anthologized, is characteristic. In it, Dickinson presents her patience and timidity—and unmasks them. In appearance a litany of instruction to her modest soul, the poem ends as an attack upon her subject. The final stroke denounces God as a traitor who demands a Judas kiss for his mercy. In light of this end, the poet's fear of judgment is revealed as a false deference before one unworthy to judge. Her consciousness that "Competing Death" may prevail spurs her, but not to penitence. Instead, she is inspired with a sense of injustice that her time is so limited. And the initial hope of Christ's appearance becomes by the end an accusation that the divine approach is far too rare. This is God the betrayer; but it is finally the poet who betrays him, who exposes his nature as unjustly hidden, prevailing upon man with unjust weapons and reigning as an unjust judge. But the poet, too, has weapons and judgments, and in this poem, it is she who prevails.

Dickinson's slow timidity, then, is present here. But it is present in all its strenuous power. She shows herself rapid and bold even in her shyness. What the poem suggests is that Dickinson, while she may be agonized, is, even more, agonistic. She actively wrestles with the problems her poetry addresses and accuses the universe of evils and contradictions she finds all too real. It further suggests her characteristic religious stance. This is one of struggle against God, whom she defies, but also toward him and with herself. For although she writes to denounce him, she invokes liturgical modes in order to do so. And God remains her subject. God is not dismissed. He continues to stand in relation to the poet's soul in contradictory assertion.

Dickinson's religious position remains an embattled one. But its importance to her work extends beyond overtly religious concerns into the fundamental technical and conceptual aspects of her poetic. Dickinson's verse forms have long attracted attention for their technical irregularities and suggest a distinct self-consciousness regarding language as a medium. Her poems typically present temporal and causal discontinuities, ateleological organizations, and irregular prosody. Examination of these formal characteristics suggests that departures from linguistic convention are a function of a growing doubt concerning traditional metaphysical sanctions for causality, teleology, and axiology. Such categories are implicit in conventional structures of articulation, as Nietzsche, for instance, points out. The possible collapse of such categories is a theme in many Dickinson poems, which present the world as it would appear without them. And it is a force governing the language of her poems, which works against sequence in time and space, against harmonies between disparate entities, and against continuous logic and full designations.

The linguistic self-consciousness implicit in Dickinson's treatment of poetic forms thus emerges as an expression of her concern with the metaphysical assumptions that promised to govern her world, but that came to seem inadequate. Metaphysical structures had purported to define the direction, order, and goal of existence— categories that remained essential to Dickinson and in terms of which she persisted in conceiving her world. Her doubts regarding these structures finally raised the whole question of linguistic meaning and of meaning in general. Her language, which reflects dissatisfaction with metaphysical systems in its configuration, finally came to address those systems, to explore directly their suppositions—and in so doing, to reflect on itself. Consciousness of language as a medium becomes consciousness of language as such, representing an increased focus on the process of signification and its possible governing principles.

Such an interest in language is not accidental. In Dickinson's tradition, the principles governing meaning had been conceived as linguistic, in terms proposed by the Logos structure. In this structure, the Logos stands between the world of eternity and that of time. Truth is identified with the former and is only accessible to the latter through a Logos that remains most strongly identified with the eternal world. Meaning, and the possibility of discourse, must rely on a positive relation between the two realms, with the transcendent world as the source and locus of significance.

In Dickinson's work, however, the two realms come to conflict; and the sanctions and structures of linguistic signification threaten to collapse. Such collapse is never quite realized in Dickinson's work. But her confrontation with it profoundly informs her conceptions of language and her poetic expression—and not only hers. The mutual implication of metaphysics and language has a particular force and clarity in her poetry. In this she is singular, but not solitary. Melville's waved fists at an enigmatic Deity; Hawthorne's sense of a resistant and incremental evil far more certain than any possible grace; Whitman's assertion of the divine self; and Emerson's proscription that the poet take up the vestments fallen from the priesthood—all trace a growing instability in metaphysical structures once secure.

This instability becomes only more pronounced in later writers with linguistic consequences already suggested by Dickinson's verse. Literary movements such as symbolism, imagism, surrealism, dadaism, futurism, and concrete poetry render Dickinson's poetic less merely eccentric. What seemed personal symptom can instead be seen as symptomatic. And Dickinson's work particularly suggests such formal experiments to be a function of metaphysical crisis which is further expressed, both by her and by later poets, in meditations on language.

Recent criticism has come increasingly to consider this question of Dickinson in relation to other writers, both of her own and of subsequent periods. Her recognition by later poets, such as the American Imagistes, and the resemblance between her verse and verse written after her have begun to suggest affinities that qualify her hitherto unquestioned isolation. Thus Karl Keller, in *The Only Kangaroo among the Beauty*, examines Dickinson's work in the context of American traditions; David Porter, in *The Modern Idiom*, does so in the context of twentieth-century modernism. And feminist criticism particularly has progressed toward examining Dickinson in less constricting terms. Studies of the social realities of nineteenth-century America and of the actual pursuits of women within it, and the stratum of such concrete experience in Dickinson's poetry have broadened the perspectives of Dickinson criticism. Treatments of her as a woman writer have the added benefit of confronting her virginity and the sexuality of her poems as active powers within her identity and as more than signs of repression, aberration, and incompletion.

These studies, however, have continued to proceed, to a greater or lesser degree, from the premise of biographical reclusion. The contours of Dickinson's world are extended beyond her own psyche, but generally little further than her literary connections. Keller's book presents Dickinson exclusively in terms of American literary history, and Porter's, in terms of literary theory. Even the feminist approach in such a work as *The Madwoman in the Attic* tends to focus on Dickinson's literary affinities at the expense of any extraliterary contacts. But the context for Dickinson's work includes more than literary influences, just as it involves more than the sphere of her own home.

Because of her seclusion, it is assumed that whatever pain Dickinson felt, whatever questions disturbed her, must be defined by a privacy into which only literature could penetrate. The possibility that her uncertainties were not self-induced, and that her concerns were not entirely private, has never been explored. Yet poem after poem suggests that the self of the poet, however imperious, is not the sole boundary of her existence nor her sole concern:

The Battle fought between the Soul
And No Man—is the One
Of all the Battles prevalent—
By far the Greater One—

No News of it is had abroad—
Its Bodiless Campaign
Establishes, and terminates—
Invisible—Unknown—   [P 594]

Dickinson's inner world is the subject of this poem. Here she depicts her personal turmoil and even particularly insists on its private nature. The soul's inner strife remains unpublicized. Yet, she declares, it is the most terrible combat. Invisible and bodiless, it is still the most bloody.

In presenting this image of inner strife, however, Dickinson does so in terms provided by the world outside her. The poem was written in 1862: the very period when Antietam and Bull Run had begun to reveal fully the horrors of the Civil War. There are in Dickinson's opus many poems that register, directly or indirectly, the civil conflagration raging around her. The notion that Dickinson's morbid fear of death and preoccupation with suffering may not have been entirely the product of her own idiosyncratic and more or less pathological imagination has never been considered. But in this poem, although Dickinson centers attention on her private world, she does so in terms drawn from the public one. The initiative even seems to lie, startling as this may be, in the public realm. The invisible and unknown struggle within the self is given a form determined by visible and known violence. Her personal conflict takes on military proportions, and in this it reflects actual events in the world of history. That the personal is foremost does not obviate the fact that, in 1862, the bodiless campaign within the poet's soul had an objective counterpart in physical and palpable warfare.

In Dickinson's work, then, metaphysical conflict is accompanied by historical trauma, and the two spheres further conjoin in a poetic remarkable for disjunctions and discontinuities. Emily Dickinson was not a librarian, remaining indoors in order to sort her reading and sift her emotions into little packets reminiscent of a card catalog. Her language, instead, records the converging crises in metaphysics and culture that can be felt in the work of other American writers and that become a profound preoccupation in writers subsequent to her. Dickinson's work presents with striking force the metaphysical revisions that so characterize modernity, as this is implicated by cultural instability and as this implicates linguistic structures. For the critique of metaphysics announced by Nietzsche has broad implications for language, which itself has a primary function and importance in traditional systems. The Logos concept, in its Johannine formulation, presented the whole possibility of intercourse between transcendence and immanence in linguistic terms. The process of signification was defined as originating in the divine Logos, and through the incarnate Logos as the avenue of its truth, as finally emerging within the immanent world. Human language was meaningful and possible only as it participated, through the Logos, in the transcendent realm. But Dickinson's work testifies to an increasing hiatus between transcendence and immanence, Logos and language. Such hiatus precipitates a conflict between human language and the traditional sources of its significance, which has only increased in strength since the time of her writing and which challenges the once accepted patterns for interpreting reality and rendering it coherent.

In Dickinson, these issues ultimately conjoin in a confrontation between the language identified with an immutable world and the immanent words of human language. The characteristic result is, in Dickinson, blasphemy:

Ended, ere it begun—
The Title was scarcely told
When the Preface perished from Consciousness
The Story, unrevealed—

Had it been mine, to print!
Had it been yours, to read!
That it was not Our privilege
The interdict of God—   [P 1088]

Dickinson's concern with language is evident in this poem. But the poem also places this concern in the metaphysical terms that consistently frame it for her. Here, a text has been interrupted. It is barely announced before its potential unfolding is engulfed: "Ended, ere it begun." Indeed, such interruption is the poem's first utterance, formally placing its own end before its beginning. The text's termination is so immediate as to seem to precede its commencement, in a profound temporal inversion.

This text takes place in the sphere of human language, which is itself identified as the poet's own world—for "Story" here figures not only as text but as universe and experience within it. This text-as-world could have been—and should have been—realized by the poet's human power, fulfilled within her human world. She would have it printed and read. But this has been willfully prevented by God's interdiction, which here has a particularly verbal resonance. God's decree forbids the completion of the human text. Divine language counters human language. What should support her utterance instead disrupts it. Nor does the poet gracefully bow to a higher, if mysterious, power. The poem is an assault. It does not declare the independence of immanent language from divine decree, but rather asserts divine decree only to attack, defame, and denounce it.

The poem thus stands poised between apostasy and affirmation—a poise that is, however, unstable and combative. There is no trace here of a timid Dickinson. The attack is frontal. And it is a linguistic attack, both as an assault through poetry and as a poem in which defiant human language strives against, but remains facing, the divine Word.

In this, Dickinson stands at the threshold of a modernity in which such struggle becomes typical. Later poets, however, could reach toward some resolution of the conflict between human and divine utterance by attempting either to reaffirm the traditional bond between them or to construct new frameworks based upon premises altogether different from the traditional ones. Dickinson, too, attempts such resolutions, but she does so without final success. She remains caught between the claims of each linguistic/metaphysical realm. The strife of this conflict, above all, informs her work. It does so not in a vacuum nor in a hermitage but in relation to the history that surrounds her. Nor does her strife render her helpless. She is furious with the God without whom she is unable to conceive her universe, but who, if responsible for a universe so incomprehensible, claims her enmity. Her poetry becomes the field of this combat with and against God. It registers, finally, the clash between his language and her own.

One

A Syntax of Contention

I am afraid we are not rid of God because we still have faith in grammar.
—Friedrich Nietzsche, *The Twilight of the Idols*

The first reviewers of Emily Dickinson's work pronounced it "bad poetry . . . divorced from meaning, from music, from grammar, from rhyme: in brief, from articulate and intelligible speech."[1] Even Dickinson's defenders conceded these all too obvious faults. Thomas Wentworth Higginson, having finally agreed to support the publication of *Poems*, did so with apologies. In his preface to the volume, he wrote, "After all, when a thought takes one's breath away, a lesson in grammar seems an impertinence."[2] Such impertinence had, however, been his. His thirty-year hesitation to recommend Dickinson's work was based on objections to form and grammar he here urges others to overlook. Even decades after the emergence of Dickinson's poems, Percy Lubbock reproached her for their "cryptic harshness, their bad rhymes and wild grammar." Harold Monro similarly complained: "Her style is clumsy, her language is poor; her technique is appalling and there is no excuse (except that very excuse of faulty technique) for the frequent elementary grammatical errors."[3]

But, as critics increasingly acknowledge, Dickinson's grammar and technique are not simply faulty, nor are they as idiosyncratic as they first appeared. Many twentieth-century writers seem equally eccentric. "Do you always have the same kind of feeling in relation to the sounds as the words come out of you or do you not. All this has much to do with grammar and with poetry and with prose," Gertrude Stein lectured in 1934.[4] She then described her lifelong struggle against the question mark, the exclamation point, and her preference for articles

1

as opposed to nouns. Dickinson's sporadic rhymes, flexible metric, and irregular syntax—what John Hollander calls her "hymnody of the attic"[5]—are features she shares with the poets who succeeded her. The similarity did not go unnoticed. As early as 1914, Harriet Monroe called Dickinson "an unconscious and uncatalogued Imagiste."[6] Amy Lowell concurred. Although Dickinson's work was "considered only as bizarre and not at all important by her contemporaries," Lowell pronounced hers the "modern" voice crying out in the literary "desert" of mid-nineteenth-century American verse.[7]

With time, Dickinson's poetry has come to seem less bizarre and more contemporary. Her syntax in particular has confirmed the modernity which the delay in her work's publication suggests. And yet, Dickinson's syntax and prosody continue to be seen as arbitrary or willfully cryptic—traits that are now identified with modernism as well. What David Porter, in his *Modern Idiom*, rightly calls Dickinson's "severe revision of transformational rules" is not, however, only a matter of "intensity" without "coherence of purpose." Porter sees Dickinson's as a "disintegration of meaning" deriving from an impulse to "act with arbitrary freedom." He sees her "defects of syntax" as "required by the constraints of the hymnal form," along with poor rhymes and a general failure of "lexical meanings." And he sees hers as a "divorce of language from the phenomenally experienced world [which] creates powerful effects characteristic of the extreme modern sensibility."

Dickinson's prosody, syntax, and figuration, however, remain expressive of her vision of reality and a serious attempt to engage its meanings. They are more than instances of "the significance of incoherence."[8] Although they certainly represent a confrontation with incoherence, they represent concomitantly a resistance to it. It is this double stress that informs Dickinson's language. What must be considered is the vision that gave rise in Dickinson to such linguistic discontinuity, the disruption of the conceptual structures necessary to give order to her world, which her language records.

Dickinson's syntax constitutes an integral part of her poetic meaning. The impulse of its disorders must be sought in the image of the world she presents. And this image is indeed a disrupted one:

Four Trees—upon a solitary Acre—
Without Design
Or Order, or Apparent Action—
Maintain—

The Sun—upon a Morning meets them—
The Wind—
No nearer Neighbor—have they—
But God—

The Acre gives them—Place—
They—Him—Attention of Passer by—
Of Shadow, or of Squirrel, haply—
Or Boy—

What Deed is Theirs unto the General Nature—
What Plan
They severally—retard—or further—
Unknown—   [P 742]

This poem presents a world of radical disorder. A scene is given, simply and in its bare particularity. The sun rises and sets over it, an eye glances at it. But there is no hint as to its place in a wider scheme. The poem does invoke a metaperspective from which the scene could be viewed as a whole, but only to declare this perspective inaccessible. Fact and a possible pattern into which it could be meaningfully placed remain disjunct. The poem is a collection of discrete details without interconnection.

Thus, in the first stanza, there are trees, there is a field, but neither of these has any relation to the other. What traffic passes is transient: a squirrel, a boy, a shadow. This last image is for Dickinson especially ominous. A shadow is, she writes elsewhere, a presentiment that darkness is about to pass (P 764), a fleeting image of the transitory. The sun and wind also frequent the field, briefly and transiently. On the other hand, the second stanza suggests the eternal and even immanent presence of the Deity, who would stand in opposition to the brief appearance and disappearance of the other elements. But even this twists as the final stanza declares him dubious company.

Instead of serving as first or final cause, tying the disparate units together, the poem closes with such a pattern absent. If God is present, he does not unite the scene. This remains a collection of isolated objects that do not cohere.

The poem's grammatical construction is as discontinuous as the scene it presents. The first, static stanza almost avoids a verb. And that verb, when it finally appears after long delay, is barely an action. Indeed, a properly transitive verb is made intransitive: "Maintain." Similarly, the final stanza circumvents a verb altogether in its main clause. The action that might have taken place is made substantive: "Deed." Only the subordinate clause has transitive verbs, and these are vague actions of even vaguer subjects: "What Plan / They severally—retard—or further—." Equally misleading is the use of an interrogative pronoun to introduce what is in fact a flat statement of lack of knowledge. "What Plan," the poet seems to ask, but she does not finally pose the question. She instead declares that the plan is unknown, an answer that is only interrogative in that it borders on accusation.

In place of any movement into which the poem's various elements can enter and mutually participate, there are series of nouns set one next to the other. These are as isolated as the solitary trees, as disconnected as general nature. In both language and nature there is lacking, and oppressive in its lack, any design that could transform this clutter into significant pattern. In these terms, the poem's syntax becomes less arbitrary. It is a function of Dickinson's sense of a world without organizing principle, a world whose parts do not cohere. Dickinson, nevertheless, hesitates to question openly an encompassing order and is reluctant to admit that she feels its lack. Her syntactic obfuscation disguises the fears of dissolution which the poem, however, traces. It expresses her doubts, even while asserting that God is indeed a "nearer Neighbor," that he oversees a design, order, or plan in general nature. The metaperspective represented by heaven and the physical world it should order remain removed from each other. No pattern emerges.

Dickinson's syntax has often attracted interpretive efforts. Brita Lindberg-Seyersted, in *The Voice of the Poet*, reviews her many oddities: incomplete sentences, ellipses of personal pronouns, relative pronouns, copulas, articles, verbs, as well as inverted or dispersed word order, ambiguous parts of speech, and strained parallel constructions.[9] Other critics treat Dickinsonian syntax and its implications in passing, particularly with regard to her conception of time.[10] Both George Whicher and James Reeves consider Dickinson's use of the conditional and the subjunctive as expressions of her uncertainty regarding the future: Whicher, because hers is a "state of chronic trepidation," and Reeves, because "truth to her is often provisional."[11] But most often, Dickinson's syntax is associated with extratemporal longings. For Charles Anderson, Dickinson's subjective and uninflected verb forms express "the desire to emphasize the absolute truth of what she was saying"; for Thomas Johnson, they "universalize her thought to embrace past, present, and future."[12]

This argument is pursued by Sharon Cameron in her book, *Lyric Time*. Cameron, like Anderson and Johnson, treats Dickinson's forms as functions of her fascination with and urge toward extratemporality. Dickinson's linguistic discontinuities are, according to Cameron, images of a wholeness which resists or negates temporal sequence. "Dickinson's utterances fragment, word cut from word, stanza from stanza, as a direct consequence of her desire for that temporal completion which will fuse all separations into the healing of a unified whole."[13] This wholeness Cameron identifies with the concept of eternity. Citing Augustine, she asserts that "lyric poems attempt such a stasis" as he describes in the *Confessions* when he envisions a "steadfast eternity, neither future nor past, [which] decrees times future and those past." And for both Augustine and Dickinson, according to Cameron, inundation by "Torrents of Eternity" is envisioned "out of desire." Rather than constituting an actual category for Dickinson, eternity is, Cameron implies, a theoretical or aesthetic concern. It is thus Dickinson's interest in "problems of temporal boundary" that leads her to be preoccupied with death: "We might regard death as a special instance of the problem of boundary, representing the ultimate division, the extreme case, the infuriating challenge to the dream of synchrony." And synchrony leads, in Dickinson's verse, to a "disjointed syntax," a "reluctance of words to totalize themselves."[14]

Dickinson's images of temporal stasis, however, often do not present the fact and idea of wholeness as Cameron claims. Nor is death a challenge to the dream of synchrony. On the contrary, Dickinson's notion of synchrony depended upon her beliefs about death and immortality. It is the challenge to those beliefs that her poetry registers. Far from representing the concordance and convergence of all temporal moments, Dickinson's instants are often temporal fragments, cut off from past and future and discordant with them. This Cameron admits. She identifies poems in which "the moment is severed from that which precedes and follows it."[15] She does not, however, distinguish between static time as fragmented time and static time as an emblem of wholeness. Only the latter can be referred to Augustine, who found in the immutable world an assurance of coherence within the world of time. In Dickinson's poetry, it is exactly this image of wholeness as rooted in the immutable world that is at issue. The question is not aesthetic, although it has aesthetic implications. What Dickinson's poetry reflects is a confusion about, not an incarnation or aesthetic displacement of, eternity.

The formal aspect of temporal/eternal relations was first recognized by Augustine himself. Kenneth Burke, in *The Rhetoric of Religion*, explicates the Augustinian construction in which "time and timelessness" correspond to "the sentence as a sequence of transitory syllables and the sentence as a fixed unit of meaning." For Augustine, that unitary meaning is an image of time endlessly extended, of a present moment "ever standing *(semper stantis)* without past or future."[16] This would seem to correlate eternity with an impulse against linguistic sequence—a correlation certainly not evident in Augustine's own work. Nor is it the case for Dickinson. Her sentence structures, when they disrupt sequence, do not necessarily signify the timelessness of eternal wholeness. The contrary is more usual. They reflect, instead, a lost sense of wholeness and consequently a sense of being lost in an extended instant which excludes, rather than includes, all past and future:

A Pit—but Heaven over it—
And Heaven beside, and Heaven abroad,
And yet a Pit—
With Heaven over it.

To stir would be to slip—
To look would be to drop—
To dream—to sap the Prop—
That holds my chances up.
Ah! Pit! With Heaven over it!

The depth is all my thought—
I dare not ask my feet—
'Twould start us where we sit
So straight you'd scarce suspect
It was a Pit—with fathoms under it—
It Circuit just the same.
Seed—summer—tomb—
Whose Doom to whom?   [P 1712]

A topography of the pit: it is situated between an above which should define it and a below which does. The poet cites a "Heaven" over and aside and abroad, and tries to situate herself in terms of its height. But she calls her position a pit, already placing it in terms of an abyss of which she is only too aware.

The poem thus tries to ward off a terror already present. The heaven that should reassure her and make her position secure does not do so. She cannot orient herself toward it and is constantly pressed by the possibility of slipping. Any movement could be a fatal upset. Even a too careful inspection of her placement could cause the whole to collapse: "To look would be to drop— / To dream—to sap the Prop." Yet the poet clearly does look and dream. She has not kept herself from gazing into the abyss below her: "The depth is all my thought." A lost sense of the world above has already made her conscious of the fathoms below, and she is suspended between the two. She therefore remains immobile, seized by fear. Her balance depends on her feeling a heaven over her—a feeling that is already tenuous and a balance that is already tottering. And she is afraid to investigate further, less the suspension collapse.

As is "Four Trees," this poem is strangely verbless. In the first stanza, prepositions dominate: *over, beside, abroad*. The pit is defined not by an action but as a space that seems vast and unfathomable and that cannot be negotiated. In this space, the poet's fear of movement is expressed through her use of conditional infinitive clauses: "To stir would be," "To look would be." All possible actions must be retained as only possible, for action could trigger the upset she fears. In the final stanza, inflected verbs do reappear—but either as the copula "is" or as denial of action: "I dare not ask." There are, as well, conditional verb forms. These are all forms of inaction. And the concluding lines even ellipse the copula. Such lack of syntactic modulation reduces the poem's thoughts and imagery to sudden conjunctions, appositions, and inversions.

In a poem whose subject is disorientation and a consequent immobility, an avoidance of verbs and a stacatto of images is not surprising. The poem's form has its source in a sense of disorientation, as Dickinson's grasp on the orders of her universe and of her place within it becomes tenuous. Such disorientation is expressed in a technique commensurate with it. Syntax mediates the sequential relations between successive words. Verb tenses place words in time relative to each other. Agreement associates parts of speech. Prepositions, copulas, and conjunctions locate, identify, and conjoin. The disruption of syntax expresses a disruption in these relations. If a sense of sequence is threatened, the result could be grammatical.

Such result is felt here, as are the sources of disruption. The poet's dislocation is referred to a heaven which does not adequately serve her as a signpost. She cannot situate herself with respect to it and therefore feels lost. Time especially disintegrates. "Seed—summer—tomb— / Whose Doom to whom?" the poet asks. The temporal circuit of birth, maturity, and death in some sense appears "just the same" as empirical perceptions. But the value of each is determined by which term is judged a "Doom." And this for Dickinson depends on heaven. If the tomb gives way to nothingness, then this world is indeed a pit and its fathoms gape wide. But if time is heaven-directed, then she is protected from such oblivion. She can feel securely placed and able to place things in turn. Which is the case, however, is exactly the question she poses. And just posing it suffices to shatter her sense of place and time.

"A Pit" therefore presents a suspended state that is not, however, an image of eternity. It is an image of paralysis. And this paralysis is referred to a threatened sense of heaven. The poem's immobility is in fact measured against and situated in terms of heaven's immutable time, the doubt of which frames it. Such paralytic instances are common in Dickinson. In "I've dropped my Brain—My Soul is numb," her veins "Stop palsied" (P 1046). "After great pain" records a similar "Hour of Lead" (P 341), as does "Pain has an Element of Blank": "Its Infinite contain / Its Past" (P 650). These are solitary moments which cannot be mistaken for concordant wholeness.

Yet wholeness is a controlling force in Dickinson's poetic, as has often been asserted. And what is implicated is the synecdochic movement that has come to be recognized as a central Dickinsonian trope. Roland Hagenbuchle's essay on "Precision and Indeterminacy in Dickinson" identifies both synecdoche and metonymy with Dickinson's characteristic suppression of subjects, causes, and contexts: "The reader is required to supply the figurative associations himself since . . . the specific referent cannot be found in the text." Hagenbuchle sees a further movement from synecdoche ("relation of inclusion") to metonymy ("relation of cause and/or association") as a figural enactment of Dickinson's "partiality for non-representational poetry," with the metonymic connections omitted.[17] Both Sharon Cameron and David Porter likewise pursue what Porter describes as a "metonymic distance from any possible origins in experience." Porter notes "the problem of the absent subject," and concurs that "there is no causation signified directly by her poems." To Porter, such figural patterns, like Dickinson's syntactic discontinuities, seem a "way of denying time or transcending it, of taking an utterance out of time."[18] Cameron too cites an elimination of cause and of context in Dickinson's poetic and similarly sees it as due to an avoidance of time inherent in the structure of lyric, but present in Dickinson in an extreme form: "The synecdochic process of taking a part for the whole, common to all poetry, is exaggerated in Dickinson's characteristic use of it in which representative incompletions are placed in a larger context of verbal incompletion, . . . pushing all utterance dangerously close to a mere word tangle. . . . [Words] refuse to totalize themselves in a context, [in a] shrinking from temporal sequence that underlies such a refusal."[19]

In Dickinson, synecdoche is a persistent figure, and its functions are a persistent concern. Effects do characteristically displace causes, which themselves remain unspecified. Antecedents are often un-named, and both the context and the source of a poem of experience are often omitted. Above all, there is a tension between parts and wholes. But what is at stake is the very possibility of relation between part and whole, between cause and effect. The purpose is not to assert fragments or to evade time. Accomplished synecdoche would do neither. By accepting a whole which parts may represent, or into which parts may be placed, both causal continuity and temporal sequence would in fact be affirmed. And this is Dickinson's desire. The incompletion that her prosody projects is, then, not a function of temporal transcendence but of its failure. And it is not a temporal evasion, except as evasion registers the failure of transcendence—the failure of wholes to contain parts and of the eternal whole to contain temporal parts, in the synecdochic movement essential to Augustin-ism. It is the effort to affirm such containment, and the ironic or desperate sense of its defeat, that determines Dickinson's synecdochic figuration:

> One Blessing had I than the rest
> So larger to my Eyes
> That I stopped gauging—satisfied—
> For this enchanted size—
>
> It was the limit of my Dream—
> The focus of my Prayer—
> A perfect—paralyzing Bliss—
> Contented as Despair—
>
> I knew no more of Want—or Cold—
> Phantasms both become
> For this new Value in the Soul—
> Supremest Earthly Sum—

One blessing is asserted, one so complete that nothing else is re-quired, so large that the very need for measure is nullified, as is the need for striving. It is both a limit and a focus at once, all-encompass-ing and wholly full. This totality, then, supercedes all parts. And it is accompanied by wholeness's attribute: cessation. But if at first its stopping seems to fulfill the prayer of immutability, by the second stanza, an ominous immobility is suggested instead. The paralysis of fragmented parts becomes indistinguishable from the immutable oneness of eternity.

The poem is thus itself posing the problem of containment, of its contours and its valence. The third stanza attempts to define these and to assert them positively. It dreams an achieved immunity from "Want—or Cold," temporality's condition which Dickinson would annul. That is, her blessing grants her the sense of eternity in which nothing passes away or is lacking. Eternity, however, the "new Value" claimed, is conceived not as some remote condition but as the "Supremest Earthly Sum." It is a totality in and of earth, not a separate estate. Wholeness is sought within the temporal condition.

Such an estate is indeed, as we will see, the limit of Dickinson's dream. An experience of immanent immortality would satisfy both her metaphysical longings and her metaphysical objections. The coherence of wholeness would be affirmed but not displaced into another world. The poem then pursues this dream of accomplished synecdoche, where the one earthly blessing would represent heaven, while heaven would include and place all earthly parts. But ultimately, the poem will acknowledge the phantasms it would dismiss, and dismiss its synecdochic dream as phantasm:

The Heaven below the Heaven above—
Obscured with ruddier Blue—
Life's Latitudes leant over—full—
The Judgment perished—too—

Why Bliss so scantily disburse—
Why Paradise defer—
Why Floods be served to Us—in Bowls—
I speculate no more—   [P 756]

The poet imagines a "Heaven below" as well as one above, the line between them obscured. This life's "Latitudes" would constitute a measureless fullness, without judgment displacing it from or into another world. This one and inclusive blessing, however, founders. Bliss is scanty. Paradise is not represented or included in terrestrial parts, but deferred beyond them. And the overflowing "Floods" of the blessing remain confined, not as fullness, but inevitably and incomprehensibly as mere part.

11

This disruption of synecdoche's mutual predication of part and whole is a characteristic Dickinsonian strategy. Many poems reach toward such positive predication, only to admit disjunction instead. In "Before I got my eye put out," the poet poses an inner vision that would contain the whole universe, but ultimately concedes that such an attempt at containment would split her apart (P 327). Elsewhere she writes: "The Heart has narrow Banks, / It measures like the Sea" (P 928), gauging her inner magnitude against an outer one. Dickinson often engages in such measurement. And often, as here, she finds that inclusive boundlessness only appears to be such, "Till Hurricane bisect" what proves to be "insufficient Area." The hurricane is itself a figure for "An instant's Push," "A Questioning." For time itself remains the challenge whose answer is an eternity undermined, in Dickinson, by questioning.

The religious dimension of Dickinsonian synecdoche is confirmed by a poetry not her own, but with which hers has intimate ties:

> My Soul forsakes her vain Delight
> And bids the World farewell;
> Base as the Dirt beneath my Feet
> and mischievous as Hell. . . .
>
> There's nothing round this spacious Earth
> That suits my large Desire;
> To boundless Joys and solid Mirth
> My nobler Thoughts aspire.
>
> Where Pleasure rolls its living Flood
> From Sin and Dross refin'd,
> Still Springing from the Throne of God,
> And fit to cheer the Mind.
>
> Th' Almighty Ruler of the Sphere,
> The glorious and the great,
> Brings his own All-sufficience there,
> To make our Bliss complete.[20]

This Isaac Watts hymn bears a strange resemblance to Dickinson's idiom. Not only the images of "Bliss" and "Flood," but the notion of wholeness which they project, are Watts's subject. Watts, too, declares a "large Desire" like Dickinson's "One Blessing"; but he une-quivocably identifies his with God. And God is defined in explicitly synecdochic terms. He is the all-sufficient, compared to whom the world is as nothing. For that wholeness which is God, all else is forsaken.

A further implication of synecdoche as a religious trope emerges here. Watts's image system seems not only synecdochic, but also paradoxical. To gain God, the world is forsaken. To fulfill the "large Desire," all earthly ones are displaced. "One Blessing" also proceeds paradoxically. The one blessing is not (or should not be) less, but more. Such paradoxes are, of course, the familiar Christian ones. To lose is to gain; to die to the self is to be reborn in Christ. To be blind to the world is to have spiritual sight. The inner soul is greater than the outer world. But these Christian paradoxes are essentially dialectical and implicitly synecdochic. Contradictory elements are synthesized into a final embracing unity, which is the ultimate gain of heaven and God. That synthetic whole, which is all-inclusive, reconciles contrary terms. Harold Bloom has pointed out the synecdochic impulses un-derlying Christian typology, in which discrete historical moments are placed into the eternal pattern of Christ's life.[21] Synecdoche similarly governs the dialectic of Christian paradox. To lose is to gain in that the ultimate whole achieved includes and places every experience, even negative ones, which have contributed to and have become part of the final, positive totality. To die to the self is in fact to realize the full self in Christ as a member of his body. Spiritual sight supercedes and subsumes all other vision.

The synecdochic pattern of Christian paradox is visible in another Watts hymn:

My God, my Portion, and my Love,
My everlasting All,
I've none but thee in Heaven above,
Or on this Earthly Ball. . . .

In vain the bright, the burning Sun
Scatters his feeble Light;
'Tis thy sweet Beams create my Noon;
If Thou withdraw, 'tis Night.

And whilst upon my restless Bed
Amongst the Shades I roll,
If my Redeemer show his Head,
'Tis Morning with my Soul. . . .

Were I possessor of the Earth,
And call'd the Stars my own,
Without thy Graces and thy self
I were a Wretch undone.

Let others stretch their Arms like Seas,
And grasp in all the Shore,
Grant me the Visits of thy Face,
And I desire no more.   [169]

Here, divine light makes night day; and sunlight, without God, is
night. To have the whole world without grace is to lose it. But grace
alone fulfills all desire. The seeming whole—the sun, the world—is in
each case exposed as mere part, which only has value when included
in and superceded by what truly is the whole. The hymn's opening is
especially suggestive. A portion of God is in fact the everlasting all; to
take part in him is to attain everything.

Dickinson, in contrast, repeatedly reaches out toward an encompassing inclusiveness, only to withdraw from the attempt as she
realizes the container will not in fact contain. Similarly, she often
posits opposites, but rarely synthesizes them in the way of dialectic,
so that thay remain opposed. The one blessing emerges not as all-
sufficient, but merely as one (and therefore, in a failed synecdoche, as
nothing). No synthetic whole reconciles contrary terms. Wholeness,
both as synecdochic and as dialectical resolution, fails to emerge,
leaving only ironic incompletion.

Yet Dickinson continues to yearn toward wholeness, whose value is
never renounced. Its continuing pressure on her is suggested by the
hymnal form itself, which so pervades her work. That Dickinson's
versification is firmly based in Isaac Watts's *Psalms, Hymns, and
Spiritual Songs* has been well demonstrated by Thomas Johnson.[22]
Dickinson's metric, accordingly, falls into the common meter of alter-
nating eight- and six-syllable lines; the long meter of eight syllables to
the line; the short meter of two lines of six syllables, followed by one of

14

eight and one of six; and variations upon them traditional to hymnody. Metric itself can be considered a "part of grammar," as Harvey Gross writes in *Sound and Form in Modern Poetry*. As such, it too "articulates relationships among objects, qualities, and actions," especially with regard to temporal orders. Metric functions as "images of time . . . grasped and understood by human awareness. . . . It is rhythm that gives time a meaningful definition, a form."[23] "One Blessing" is itself a poem in common meter. The introduction of the hymnal mode, associated as this must be with affirmations of faith, in a poem of disruption is noteworthy. It opens the general question of the tensions implicit in her use of hymnody to express not faith but uncertainty, with the confusion and hostility this gave rise to in Dickinson's mind.

This tension is particularly evident in a poem whose subject, diction, and metric is decisively hymnal, but whose purport is a denial of doubt which argues its presence:

My Faith is larger than the Hills—
So when the Hills decay—
My Faith must take the Purple Wheel
To show the Sun the way—

'Tis first He steps upon the Vane—
And then—upon the Hill—
And then abroad the World He go
To do His Golden Will—

And if His Yellow feet should miss—
The Bird would not arise—
The Flowers would slumber on their Stems—
No Bells have Paradise—

How dare I, therefore, stint a faith
On which so vast depends—
Lest Firmament should fail for me—
The Rivet in the Bands—   [P 766]

A consistent common meter prevails in this poem, whose opening figure is especially hymnlike. It declares a faith greater than the greatest natural phenomena and implies an ascent from things of nature to things of spirit. Hills and sun stand as emblems of eternity. And if hills do alter, the sun's circuit assuredly never fails. This first stanza does introduce dissonant notes. "When the Hills decay" assumes deterioration to be nature's most salient trait—and only Dickinson's expert eye could see in the millennial process of geological change an instance of the transitory. Even the sun, adopted as a more secure figure of eternity, is somewhat acknowledged to be, in this, figural. Faith must still "take the Purple Wheel" and "show the sun" its way toward symbolizing permanence. Nevertheless, the first stanza argues for some movement from the perception of nature's objects to intimations of immortality.

The poem thus accepts its own figure of eternity and in the second stanza joins omnipresence to sempiternity. The sun's circuit encompasses vane and hill and the world at large. It is only in the third stanza that the dissonant note emerges into prominence. The sun figure comes to signal, through negativity, not an immutable order but a pressing sense of its possible failure. The sun's stride might break; its circuit comes to suggest an image of eternity confounded. With its overthrow falls every other process: in nature, as seen metonymically in the failure of birds to return and flowers to bloom, and in supernature, with the silencing of heaven's bells. This last image is in fact redundant. It is the failure of heaven that the sun's broken movement signals and that has priority. As the final stanza demonstrates, what is at issue is the faith in heaven's immutability. It is this that determines the poet's perception of all orders in nature, the sun among them.

This final stanza in some sense reasserts the hymnal stance of the poem's opening. But it does so in contrary fashion. Faith is not so much affirmed as declared necessary. The poet cannot dare to "stint" her belief in the everlasting, lest the admission of heaven's failure unleash all the forces of dissolution she thus far only suspects to be ascendant in her world. "Firmament" is, for her, the "Rivet in the Bands." A belief in eternity is what holds all things together. Its breaking apart would dissolve all else. The hymnal metric is, therefore, not merely ironic. The poem's statement verges on unfaith and a palpable sensing of its consequences. But it draws back from apostasy. The regular common meter continues to assert the organization and regularity which the poet never quite relinquishes.

Dickinson's forms are therefore more closely involved with conflict than they are linguistic representations of wholeness, although they attempt to retain their grasp on wholeness—one origin, in fact, of their conflict. They raise, above all, the question of temporal orders. That Dickinson's relation to time was highly problematic has often been discussed. Clark Griffith, for example, in *The Long Shadow*, argues that Dickinson found her world overwhelmingly threatening, cruel, and chaotic:

> In her poetry, nature is capable of conferring moments of great ecstasy. But the moments prove fleeting and transitory. They tantalize the observer, lull her feelings into false security. Suddenly, they pass, to be followed by periods when nature glares back with a chilling hostility.[24]

This spectacle of impermanence terrified Dickinson. Nature seemed to her, as Allen Tate points out, a disintegrating force characterized by corruption and decay.[25] Time passes, things change, and above all, they die. Dickinson had a profound sense of time's transiency and found it exceedingly alarming. "I feel that life is short and time fleeting, and that I ought now to make my peace with my maker," she wrote in one of her earliest letters.[26] Soon after, she again wrote, "We take no note of time, but from its loss" (L 13). As in "My Faith is larger than the Hills," nature could not provide her with an assurance of stability. It, instead, suggested to her the possibilities of constancy's default. To her, time represented in its motion the very epitome, not only of loss, but of deception. Its beauties and its joys were nothing more than mere vanishing semblances. To her, then, "Day" was composed of:

A morning and a noon
A Revelry unspeakable
And then a gay unknown
Whose Pomps allure and spurn
And dower and deprive
And penury for Glory
Remedilessly leave.   [P 1675]

Morning and noon here do not merely pass away. They betray and delude, so that even their positive beauties are subverted and finally negated. The gay revelry, even when announced, is already revoked as "unspeakable" and "unknown." What initially seems to be terms of Emersonian ecstasy—welcoming "as it were in flashes of light . . . sudden discoveries of profound beauty and repose" even if they are fleeting—are here deflationary.[27] The ascent is in fact descent. The pomps spurn even as they allure; the sequence of "dower and deprive" which the sun's diurnal arc traces for the poet is not even linear, but a simultaneous undermining. In the end, glory has not only been displaced by but is shown to have never been anything but a penury without remedy.

Against this spectacle of change and loss, Dickinson opposed eternity. Her whole ability to comprehend time was eternity-dependent and was so in several senses. To Dickinson, eternity was a unitary, immutable other world, standing beyond time as both its end and its totality. As such, it determined her primary conceptual categories: causality, axiology, teleology. Eternity as the end of time provided the telos toward which every moment was directed, in terms of which the position and importance of every moment relative to other moments could be established, and within which, as within an inclusive sum, every event would take its place. Eternity thus guaranteed the sequence, value, and purpose of the temporal process—and of the linguistic process as well. For through these causal, axiological, and teleological categories Dickinson not only structured but also ultimately articulated her world. Dickinson's verse dramatizes her dependence on eternity with regard to each of these conceptual categories and reflects, in its formal fissures, the consequences of doubting them for both perceptual and linguistic orders. Eternity thus emerges as a center of contention. Without it, the dissolution so often attributed to her work would indeed ensue. She therefore struggled incessantly to retain not only a notion of but a faith in eternity. It is the tension between the threat of disorder, which the doubt of eternity represented, and the inability to dispel such doubt altogether, which her language registers.

First, Dickinson's sense of causal coherence was derived from her belief in an immutable world. She saw the end of time as providing a vantage point from which to look back on life's discrete events and in terms of which those events could be placed in sequence. They would become linked in perceivable succession, and the pattern through which each moment leads into the next would become evident. "Retrospection," she writes, "is Prospect's half" (P 995). Retrospect in fact makes prospect possible. The ability to negotiate time progressively depends upon a belief that on review all the different events will be situated:

> The Admirations—and Contempts—of time—
> Show justest—through an Open Tomb—
> The Dying—as it were a Height
> Reorganizes Estimate
> And what We saw not
> We distinguish clear—
> And mostly—see not
> What We saw before—
>
> 'Tis Compound Vision—
> Light—enabling Light—
> The Finite—furnished
> With the Infinite—
> Convex—and Concave Witness—
> Back—toward Time—
> And forward—
> Toward the God of Him—   [P 906]

As in so many poems, Dickinson projects forward to an ultimate stance (often, as here, that of death) in order to project back to her present moment—now seen, however, from a posterior viewpoint. Dickinson, that is, would read time backwards. She attempts to establish her moments as at once viewed and reviewed. She thus "Reorganizes Estimate" from the backward stance of the tomb. From the end, we see "what We saw not" and do not see "What we saw before." Then, time and eternity, the finite and infinite, together form a "Compound Vision." Time, seen retrospectively, emerges as a continuum forward toward the God who directs it. With such a retrogressive progression, the relative place of each moment emerges into cohesive shape.

The relative value of each moment emerges as well. "Admirations" become distinguished from "Contempts." Each event is not only organized and integrated but also weighed and judged. The tomb is more than the last point in a continuum from which to look back. It constitutes and encompasses all time at once. Not just end, but end as synecdochic wholeness provides the retrospective stance that makes forward motion possible and that determines its axiology. And only such final totality allows time's "Contempts" to be borne. The temporal differentiation that Dickinson found so unacceptable and that seemed a continual incremental loss would be justified only if it were a function of temporal wholeness. "Chaos" is described in one poem as a voyage in which there is not "even a Report of Land— / To justify—Despair" (P 510). Without terminus, the journey seems senseless; and terminus must, as well, be validating. Final stance finally serves as the only redemption from traumas which Dickinson felt to be absolute, even as they were daily:

> The Days that we can spare
> Are those a Function die
> Or Friend or Nature—stranded then
> In our Economy
>
> Our Estimates a Scheme—
> Our Ultimates a Sham—
> We let go all of Time without
> Arithmetic of him— [P 1184]

Loss of function, friend, or nature, all inevitable, will deprive the poet of sequence, unmask her judgments as mere schemes, and declare her "Ultimates" to be sham endings and sham values that neither explain nor justify—unless she have an "Arithmetic" of time. Time's arithmetic, an impressive figure for prosody, here entails the totality that governs linguistic and empirical pattern. On it, Dickinson's ability to compute, comprehend, and evaluate duration depends. Without it, duration scatters, leaving the poet stranded.

Both the coherence and values eternity bestows are in turn aspects of a teleological framework which establishes the purpose of events. Frank Kermode, in *The Sense of an Ending*, posits teleological formulation as a human imperative. "There is still a need to speak humanly of a life's importance in relation to it," writes Kermode, "a need in the moment of existence to belong, to be related to a beginning and to an end." And, in the traditional Christian structure, the end was identified with a world of Being, of Divinity, of timeless unity, against which the world of time was measured: "We have a creation of which the law relating to forms is a law of change and succession, and a Creator whose realm and forms are changeless and non-successive."[28] Their interrelation becomes centered on the end point at which they merge or on the particular moments in time that may serve as teleological emblems.

It is in moving toward a telos that experience achieves, for Dickinson, both logical succession and value. Her "inclination toward aftermath" is therefore not "simply an unexplained but persistent leaning."[29] It is integral to her conceptual grasp of reality's structure as it is integral to her poetic structure—which is why Dickinson's poems must so often be read backwards from their end. And it is as telos that Dickinson's eternity ultimately functions:

Each Life Converges to some Centre—
Expressed—or still—
Exists in every Human Nature
A Goal—

Embodied scarcely to itself—it may be—
too fair
For Credibility's presumption
To mar—

Adored with caution—as a Brittle Heaven—
To reach
Were hopeless, as the Rainbow's Raiment
To touch—

Yet persevered toward—sure—for the Distance—
How high—
Unto the Saints' slow diligence—
The Sky—

Ungained—it may be—by a Life's low Venture—
But then—
Eternity enable the endeavoring
Again.   [P 680]

The progressive qualification of this poem only dramatizes the poet's need for its assertions. The poem opens with a positive declaration—"Exists in every Human Nature / A Goal"—but each subsequent stanza qualifies this statement. The goal is "Embodied scarcely to itself." "Credibility's presumption" could "mar" it, for it is not easily believed. It must be "Adored with caution." "To reach" it "Were hopeless." But in spite of qualification, the goal is "persevered toward." The fourth stanza seems to move beyond hesitation into reaffirmation. The sky is then attained, through whatever distance, by the "Saints' slow diligence," and the final stanza specifies the hope that makes the effort possible. Even if the goal remains beyond life's reach, eternity will "enable the endeavoring / Again."

This conclusion would be more convincing if the poet had not, in the poem's course, presented both goal and eternity as unattainable, as hopeless to reach as would be a rainbow. The relation between goal and process remains complicated: complications in which the poem's prosody shares. This enacts the tension between goal and process. Each stanza delays its syntactic completion until its end and only then is its sense apparent: "Exists . . . A Goal . . . Credibility's presumption to mar." In each case, subject and complement are inverted, so that the intention is hidden until the end. Even then the statement is not always clear. And the strange spondees at each stanza's end, comprising the poem's only metrical regularity, serve to emphasize these conclusions of thought, while against the stanzas' rhythmic alterations, they do not quite establish any conclusive regularity.

This prosody underscores the goal as that which governs process. It also underscores how tenuous relations between goal and process can be. Syntactically, inverted complements lead to confusion as to the subject left behind; conceptually, the significance of what has gone before depends entirely upon an end that remains beyond it and that remains unknown. Life's close may in fact be closure, a cessation of time rather than its completion. This makes the end suspect. "Advance is Life's condition," the poet writes, and the "Grave but a Relay." But it may be that the grave is in fact a "terminus," and then it is "hated" (P 1652). And were the grave indeed terminus, all process would disintegrate for Dickinson. In "Each Life," the uncertain proceeding and confusion as to ends show the space that could open between them, even as the poem gropes toward assertion of process governed by end.

But poems that retain a sense of ending, while foreseeing in their structure the possibility of its collapse, give way to poems in which such a collapse does occur. The poet is then faced with a chaos that inundates and a complete loss of sequence. She experiences what it is like to venture "Down Time's quaint stream / Without an oar," what it is like to sail with "Our Port a secret / Our Perchance a Gale" (P 1656). All is arbitrary, and no known end guides. Temporal definition is then lost. The poet, finding that her "Sum" has fallen into "schism," finds that she has "wrecked the Pendulum" (P 1569). Spatial definition is likewise effaced. Experience becomes a "Boundlessness" whose "Location is Illocality" (P 963). Infinity is no longer a redeeming but a disorienting realm:

> From Blank to Blank—
> A Threadless Way
> I pushed Mechanic feet—
> To stop—or perish—or advance—
> Alike indifferent—
>
> If end I gained
> It ends beyond
> Indefinite disclosed—
> I shut my eyes—and groped as well
> 'Twas lighter—to be Blind—   [P 761]

The end cited here is conditional and transforms "beyond" from a designation of place—the other world—into "beyond" as a dependent and indefinite adjective: beyond what the poet can gauge. But without the reference point provided by an end, movement becomes impossible. Movement necessarily entails measure, a distance negotiated from one point to another. Here, however, instead of points, there are blanks. Thus motion can only be "Threadless," without delineation. Neither stopping nor advancing nor even perishing can be distinguished, because all relations that could define them have been lost. The poem concludes with a subtle Dickinsonian inversion of the familiar religious paradox by which external darkness may be spiritually bright.[30] Writes Isaac Watts:

My God, my Life, my Love,
To thee, to thee I call.
I cannot live if thou remove,
For thou art all in all.

Thy shining Grace can cheer
This Dungeon where I dwell;
'Tis Paradise when thou art here,
If thou depart, 'tis Hell.   [170]

Here darkness is subsumed into the experience of God's totality, the spiritual illumination which cancels all blindness. But in Dickinson the religious dialectic breaks apart. Blindness is not paradoxically vision. When space has no definition, to see or not become functional equivalents—except that blindness raises no doomed expectations. Blindness is therefore chosen, but as a darkness which remains itself: an incomplete dialectic unsynthesized into any all-inclusive divine light.

The loss of wholeness threatened here finally comes to be defined by Dickinson as a place of despair:

No Man can compass a Despair—
As round a Goalless Road
No faster than a Mile at once
The Traveller proceed—

Unconscious of the Width—
Unconscious that the Sun
Be setting on His progress—
So accurate the One

At estimating Pain—
Whose own—has just begun—
His ignorance—the Angel
That pilot Him along—   [P 477]

Despair is a "Goalless Road" along which the traveler proceeds but has no sense of progression. He travels unaware of distance as marked by the sun in a space without demarcation. Only the pain that comes with loss of direction serves to measure his movement and comprises the space of his journey. In this space, advance is impossible. The way is circular, and even if he hurried he could never complete it. A goalless road cannot be compassed, for it has no end.

In fear of finding herself in the untraversable space of such despair, Dickinson stops short of a declared unbelief in ends or in the structure that provided her with a teleology. Outright rejection of her faith would thrust such dislocation upon her. She therefore tries to retain her hold upon belief. Yet firm belief continues to elude her. The "Angel" of her journey thus remains, if not apostasy, then "Ignorance." But even uncertainty acts as a "pilot" toward the realm of dissolved limits which the poet tries to resist.

This mediate position gives rise in Dickinson to conflicting and often contradictory statements, which have caused her to be categorized in turn as a mystic and as an apostate. She is, on the one hand, included among ecstatic if unorthodox poets "filled with love for the beauty they perceive in the world of time," and who are "neither fearful nor morbid in facing death."[31] Or, in a more orthodox manner, she is said to have discovered herself "elected to receive the grace of God."[32] On the other hand, the religious doubts she so often expresses has led her to be seen as having renounced her faith and, most often, replaced it with a belief in her own powers, especially those employed in her art. She is then said to have embraced poetry, in the Arnoldian mode, in religion's stead. Heaven becomes for her a "poetic faith";[33] "Imagination's fictions rescue the world."[34]

Even Albert Gelpi, who recognizes Dickinson's ambivalence, sees it as finally resolved in a transferral from a reliance on heaven to a reliance on the self. He notes that Dickinson referred to herself as both a "pagan" and a "Puritan spirit" and discusses at length in *The Mind of the Poet* her inability to accept wholeheartedly the theological inheritance of New England while remaining under its influence. But, according to Gelpi, "lack of commitment to external absolutes drove the search within, pivoted the mind to turn and turn upon itself." As a result, "her basic motive—the highest motive that the will could command—was comprehension: to know and feel as intensely as possible."[35]

Dickinson, however, never lost her commitment to external absolutes, nor were intense knowledge and feeling her motives. She could not accept a personal and subjective meaning as substitute for an external one operating through objective creation. If the world lacked order, then so did her personal existence. A dispassionate exploration for the sake of abstract knowledge hardly corresponds to the urgency of her poetry. Gelpi is correct in refuting the claims of biographers that "passing years and the death of friends forced a serene acceptance of immortality." But his assertion that "much of the time she would have been satisfied with the stoicism . . . which neither feared extinction nor prized redemption" assumes a resolution to a conflict never resolved.[36] Emily Dickinson feared extinction. She prized redemption. She desperately wished for some assurance that the passing of time was an orderly process and that apparent dissolution was in truth a patterned unfolding. About this she was neither serene nor stoic.

Dickinson's therefore remained a "religion / That doubts as fervently as it believes" (P 1144).[37] She was poised between a faith she could not embrace and an apostasy too terrible to be finally asserted. In a very early letter, she had already described this condition. Identifying herself with the Satan of Job, she felt left to "Pause, and ponder, and ponder, and pause, and do work without knowing why—not surely for this brief world, and more sure it is not for heaven." Unable to accept heaven, she was left only with this brief world, which, however, without heaven, seemed a dreadful place indeed. Thus, in the same letter, she returned to belief:

> What shall we do when trial grows more, and more, when the dim lone light expires, and it's dark, so very dark, and we wander, and know not where, and cannot get out of the forest—whose hand to help us, and to lead, and forever guide us, they talk of a "Jesus of Nazareth," will you tell me if it be he? [L 36]

Dickinson's doubts tempted her to forsake God. But her needs impelled her toward faith in him. Neither stance could triumph, but they could not be reconciled.

"Christian eternity," writes Octavio Paz, "was the solution to all contradictions and anguish, the end of history and of time."[38] Modern conceptions of time have accepted the rectilinear and irreversible temporal scheme of the Christian model. But it has eliminated both creator and end. Paz cites Jean Paul's *Dream: Speech of Christ, from the Universe, That There is No God* in this shift of temporal archetype. In contrast with the Enlightenment attack on Christianity, which still "postulated the existence of a universal order" and believed that "an intelligent necessity, divine or natural, moved the world," Jean Paul sees contingency and unreason as a result of the death of God. He does not accept a mechanistic universe. His world is convulsive: "The universe is chaos because it has no creator." Paz compares this vision with the dark night of the mystics, in which we feel "adrift, abandoned in a hostile or indifferent world." But, he adds, it is a night without end. The rejection of an eternal world in which all things achieve their absolute state, for good or evil, and of the God who orders the created world in terms of these absolutes threatens to transform cosmos into chaos. And the modern age has rejected the eternal world. Paz defines modernity as an age of criticism, especially in its tendency to criticize the Christian temporal archetype: "Christianity postulated an abolution of the future by conceiving of eternity as the place of perfection. Modernity begins as a criticism of Christian eternity."[39]

In Emily Dickinson, the beginning of this criticism is apparent. And she is aware of its consequences. Her whole sense of coherence, of meaning, and of purpose in the world depended upon the Christian schema in which all things move toward a meaningful end. Earth and heaven should form a pattern that encompasses all experience. This pattern meant, for Dickinson, the difference between chaos and order. But the parts of the pattern would not fit together. Eternity remained a mystery her faith could not penetrate. Consequently, she saw before her an abyss of utter confusion:

> More than the Grave is closed to me—
> The Grave and that Eternity
> To which the Grave adheres—
> I cling to nowhere till I fall—
> The Crash of nothing, yet of all—
> How similar appears—   [P 1503]

Dickinson here does not reject Christian eternity. Her critique does not draw conclusions. Nor does she declare the death of God. But she is uncertain about his presence. The grave, with all its secrets, is closed to her. Her faith cannot quite negotiate the distance between life and death. And she has glimpsed the crash that would follow a complete loss of faith. In this, she glimpses the vision of Nietzsche's madman who, in *The Gay Science*, raves about the death of God:

> Whither are we moving now? Away from all suns? Are we not plunging continually? Backward, sideward, forward, in all directions? Is there any up or down left? Are we not straying as through an infinite nothing? Do we not feel the breath of empty space?[40]

Emily Dickinson, even from uncertainty rather than apostasy, feels this breath of empty space. She feels its disorientation and knows that if it becomes her vision, she will be lost in a world without backward or forward or any direction. She will cling to nowhere and fall through nothing.

The disorientation Dickinson here senses becomes, after Nietzsche, a familiar vision. Dickinson shares with her successors a critical attitude toward inherited metaphysical frameworks, an attitude her forms register. Nietzsche himself had considered the relation between our language and our conceptual categories. "The basic presuppositions of the metaphysics of language" he considers especially to involve causality, with its "concept of transcendent being everywhere projected by thought." And Nietzsche suggests that these are supported above all by our linguistic habits: "After all, every word we say and every sentence speak in its favor."[41] In Dickinson's work, sentences no longer speak in its favor with the same force. Dickinson does not deny the metaphysical world or the structures built upon it. But she admits the possibility of such denial. And for her, this threatens to transform the cosmos into a space empty of significance, as the motions of the heavens lead her to an overwhelming question:

> The Moon upon her fluent Route
> Defiant of a Road—
> The Star's Etruscan Argument
> Substantiate a God—
>
> If Aims impel these Astral Ones
> The ones allowed to know
> Know that which makes them as forgot
> As Dawn forgets them—now—   [P 1528]

This poem begins with empirical observation. The lunar path appears "Defiant of a Road," arbitrary, following no appointed route. As to the stars, if their movements "Substantiate" a divine order—and the verb tense remains conditional with an ellipse of the modal "might"—the "Argument" remains "Etruscan." Etruscan, says the dictionary, is the extinct language of Etruria, not known to be related to any other language. Thus, the star's message, if it attests the existence of God, cannot be understood; and the order this would imply remains invisible to the poet. The facts, as they are perceived by the unprejudiced eye, do not necessarily support a belief in divine supervision of the universe.

The second stanza moves into a conditional assessment of the perceived facts. The sidereal movements may have a purpose. They may not be simply random. But if not, the knowledge is restricted and is not accessible to us. As to who may be in possession of it, the poem is ambiguous. The inverted sentence order and unspecified pronoun of the opening lines only confuse. "The ones allowed to know" may be the "Astral Ones," the stars themselves, whom dawn "forgets" as day eclipses the night sky. But elsewhere Dickinson had written of the dead soul: "Even Nature herself / Has forgot it is there" (P 1344). The ones who are "as forgot" may be the dead, whom "Dawn," the living day, forgets in their eternal night. The dead have been initiated into the mystery of eternity. This is the mystery on which the aim of the stars ultimately depends, and the dead may know the answer to the question posed by the universe. But whether the stars or the dead are possessors of this knowledge, it remains their exclusive property. Those who live on earth must continue to question. Nevertheless, except for the initiating "If" of the stanza, this would be a statement of faith. At least heavenly beings know. But the stanza is set in the conditional and remains a hypothetical statement of a possible answer to which, in any event, the living have no access.

Dickinson is questioning here all those assumptions about time, order, and aim without which her universe becomes inconceivable. The mere suspension of faith in teleology and theology, which is implicit in the empirical first stanza and the conditional second stanza, represents a threat of disintegration. This threat is reflected in the poem's language. George Steiner, in his writings, is repeatedly concerned with the way in which "syntax mirrors or controls the reality concept" of a given culture:

> So much of that characteristic Western sense of time as vectored flow, of sequential causality, of the irreducible status of the individual, is inseparable from the bone structure, from the lucid . . . patterns of Indo-European syntax. We can locate in these patterns the substrata of past-present-future, of subject-verb-object, of pronomial disjunction between ego and collectivity that shape so many elements in Western metaphysics, religion, and politics.[42]

A cohesive sentence structure posits and reflects a belief in time as a sequential, causal continuum, and in space as an integrated, interrelating system. In this poem, sentence structure is savaged, with its ellipses of the copula and modal auxiliaries of verbs, inversions of sentence order, and persistent ambiguities. If the sense of time as "vectored flow" and "sequential causality" is, as Steiner suggests, inseparable from the "lucid patterns of Indo-European syntax," this tortuous syntax suggests a challenge to such coherence, as does the poem's argument.

"The Moon upon her fluent Route" looks forward to the era initiated by Nietzsche. It peers into the vision of aimlessness and disorder which Nietzsche made his theme. Its language is consequent to that vision in its fragmentation, its disruption of sequence, and, not least, its linguistic imagery. Dickinson proposes, as does the Nineteenth Psalm, a linguistic trope for heavenly motion. The lunar orbit is a "fluent Route," the astral pattern is an "Estruscan Argument." But, unlike the psalmist, Dickinson implies that they are so in a code difficult to decipher. This shift to a universe conceived as linguistic, like the poem's language, can be seen as part of the reassessment of metaphysical assumptions the poem implies. Its epistemological problems ultimately raise questions concerning the processes of signification within linguistic systems, with an increased attention on language as a realm in its own right. In this, Dickinson heralds the universe of modern poetry, which is increasingly linguistic even as its forms are increasingly difficult.

For Dickinson, traditional explanations no longer quite explain, and the world, therefore, threatens to become inexplicable. The model of eternal wholeness, of concordant time, becomes for her problematic as a paradigm for the temporal unfolding that is essentially different from it but that is, for her, dependent upon it. And if order depends upon eternity as end, the doubt of it could lead to order's collapse. In Dickinson's forms, the effects of such a possible collapse are felt; in her poetry and her poetic, its causes can be traced, as can her attempts either to reaffirm her inherited teleology or to conceive an alternative one.

Dickinson's language thus reflects both her need to affirm structures for her world and her recognition that traditional structures had grown insecure, which she shares with later writers. Her own attempts to erect new structures from or instead of those available to her remained, to a great degree, a struggle between acceptance and rejection of the beliefs she had inherited. The difficulty of her verse reflects this struggle and is no less accidental than the difficulty of the verse written after her. Because of her tantalizing reclusion, critics tend to overlook objective contexts for Dickinson's work. At most, some relate her religious uncertainty to a general transition in American Calvinism, and these still focus on her personal religious sensibility. Emily Dickinson was certainly the most private of poets. But if her beliefs were shaken, this is because her world shook them. For her period, not unlike our own, was characterized by change, instability, and above all, war.

Two

Political Theology

There is no remoteness of life and thought, no hermetically sealed seclusion, except, perhaps, that of the grave, into which the disturbing influences of this war do not penetrate.
                —Nathaniel Hawthorne, "Chiefly about War Matters"

Religious conflict has long been recognized as an important factor in Emily Dickinson's work. Her seclusion, too, has been given much attention. But these are treated as isolated phenomena. Her beliefs, her life, and her poetry are seen as the affairs of a private mind in a private world, which remains shrouded in mystery. The causes of her withdrawal continue to be perplexing. Its relation to her work remains obscure. Equally obscure is the nature of the "poetic drive" that produced the bulk of her work in a few years and then was, as Thomas Johnson describes it, "suddenly at an end."[1] Although recent attempts have been made to relate these personal circumstances to external conditions, Dickinson's image as unaware of, or unconcerned with, actual events taking place beyond her father's gate more or less persists.

Dickinson's indifference to all wordly affairs, however, was neither as complete nor as straightforward as has been traditionally assumed. Johnson identifies the abrupt decline in Dickinson's poetic production with the year 1866. He identifies the "rising flood of her talent" with the years 1858–61, the years during which her reclusive tendencies also began to emerge. And the proposed chronology of the 1,656 poems that have been given approximate dates reveals that 852 poems, over half of Dickinson's entire opus, were written between 1861 and 1865. These are, of course, the years of the Civil War in America, a coincidence that has never been fully assessed.

The exact effects the war may have had on Dickinson are difficult to determine, just as it is difficult to determine its exact effects upon other American writers. That Dickinson's case was rather exceptional cannot be denied. While only Whitman, of the northern writers, became what can be called directly involved in the war's events, only Dickinson entirely refused to emerge from her own home. Hawthorne, however, spent the decade preceding the war's outbreak in the Liverpool consulship; on his return to the United States, he retired to New England. With the exception of one trip to Washington, undertaken for reasons of health, he had no personal exposure to actual war scenes. Emerson similarly remained in New England, with a visit to the Charleston Navy Yard as his most immediate contact with army life. And Melville had, by the war's outbreak, already commenced what one critic calls his "strategic withdrawal toward that custom house existence which he learned so tenaciously to lead."[2] One visit to the Brooklyn Naval Yard and one to Vienna, Virginia, to visit with a cousin constituted his direct war experiences.

In comparison with other northern writers, then, Dickinson's removal from events was, although extreme, one of degree. While the extremity should not be overlooked, neither should a historical situation be entirely denied Dickinson. The other writers of the North felt, from their differing exposures, more or less direct responses to the war. Into this range of response Dickinson's work should also be placed. The war framed her attitudes and efforts, as it did those of other writers. It became for her, as it did for them, an arena for the clash of beliefs and doubts, with concerns long held given through war a greater urgency. It may thus be said of Dickinson, as Henry James said of himself, that the war stood as a "quite indescribably intensified time—intensified through all lapses of occasion and frustrations of contact; . . . although the case had to be in a peculiar degree, alas, that of living inwardly."[3]

Regarding Dickinson, however, the undeniable inwardness has eclipsed any possible intensity. Most biographers simply dismiss the subject of the Civil War. Richard Sewall does review some of the circumstances by which the war touched Dickinson's life but restricts its effect on her to the elegies she wrote in memory of the Amherst war dead.[4] In the single published article devoted to "Emily Dickinson and the Civil War," Thomas Ford notes that the war was Dickin-

33

son's most creative period. This he attributes to the fact that "casualties in battle acted to increase her awareness of death, which in turn roused her creative energies."[5] Ford then proposes four poems as directly deriving from the war. Daniel Aaron includes Dickinson in *The Unwritten War,* but does so only in a supplement and mainly to reiterate her isolation. Even recent studies, in which broader contexts for Dickinson's work have begun to be explored, have rarely ventured beyond her literary affinities. Karl Keller, in his study of Dickinson in her American context insists on "her existence outside/apart from action in history" and asserts that there are "few poetic references to the Civil War" in her work. David Porter, in his study of Dickinson in the context of literary modernism similarly insists that there is "no Civil War in the flood of poems from the war years."[6] Even *The Madwoman in the Attic* presents her as a "nun, buried alive in her own society."[7]

Dickinson's work should, however, be placed, not only within the intellectual and literary currents of her period, but also into the realm of concrete historical events. When considered as part of the history shared with her contemporaries, Dickinson can emerge from her supposed indifference to any world but her private one, while many of the eccentricities of her vision come to seem less merely self-generated.

Every circumstance of Dickinson's social existence argues against her utter detachment from public affairs. The Dickinson family had a tradition of involvement in civic life, commencing with her grandfather, who was a founder of Amherst College, and continuing with her father and her brother. Both Edward and Austin Dickinson served as treasurer of the college. Both headed town meetings and civic projects. Edward brought the railroad to Amherst and became president of it, directed the Home Mission Society, and was a trustee of the Northampton hospital. Austin served on the library board, the board of Amherst Academy, the Village Improvement Association. He promoted and supervised the building of the First Church of Amherst.[8]

Nor were the Dickinson activities restricted to Amherst. In 1838, Edward Dickinson was elected representative to the General Court of Massachusetts. He was delegate to the National Whig convention in 1852 and in the same year was elected to the United States Congress.

Far from being removed from the main current of events in the town and in the nation, Emily Dickinson lived in an atmosphere of political commitment and controversy. Her father's term in Washington spanned the period of the Kansas-Nebraska Act, the Fugitive Slave Act, and the first attempts to found a new party, out of which the Republican party later emerged. (One meeting to discuss this issue was held in the rooms shared by Edward Dickinson and Thomas D. Eliot—granduncle to another American poet.)[9]

Emily Dickinson's home was far from cloistered. Her circle of acquaintance was no less unsheltered and unsheltering. Samuel Bowles, one of Dickinson's correspondents of many years, was editor of the *Springfield Republican* and a political figure of national importance. Dr. Josiah Holland, another close friend, was a columnist for the *Springfield Republican*, an editor of *Scribner's Magazine*, and wrote one of the first biographies of Lincoln. And Thomas Wentworth Higginson, Dickinson's main literary correspondent, was a leading activist in the antislavery and the women's rights movements. He was a colonel in the Union Army and was an officer of its first black regiment when Dickinson began writing to him.

Dickinson not only knew these journalists and activists, she also read their publications. Jack Capps, in *Emily Dickinson's Reading*, reports that the Dickinson household subscribed to the *Springfield Republican*, the *Hampshire and Franklin Express*, the *Amherst Record*, as well as to *Harper's New Monthly*, *Scribner's*, and the *Atlantic Monthly*. Dickinson's letters frequently refer to births, marriages, and deaths reported in the *Republican* as well as to news items. Her knowledge of Higginson's whereabouts throughout the war years derived from notices in the *Republican*. *Harper's* supplemented the *Republican* for news. Each issue included a "Monthly Record of Current Events" and editorials on public affairs. Between her family, her friends, and her journals, Dickinson in her room was better informed and closer to political circles than are most people under less constrained circumstances.

This existence in a politically charged atmosphere, at a time of national crisis, with family and friends actively involved in public affairs, is reflected in both Dickinson's letters and her verse. Much of her correspondence is missing, and many passages from letters have been excised. Nevertheless, of the seventy-five letters thought to have been written between 1861 and 1865 (and some of these are bare notes to Susan Gilbert Dickinson next door), at least fifteen directly refer to the war.[10] Some remarks are incidental. There are passing allusions to soldiers (L 235, 272, 279) or to political events. Dickinson mentions the rivalry between "straight Whigs" and "republican Whigs" (L 240), Lincoln's reelection (L 297), and Jefferson Davis's capture (L 308). Some letters mourn the fate of personal acquaintances (L 245, 255, 256, 257); but others show a wider concern. Dickinson's attention was not restricted to the safety of those she knew. It extended to the general framework of war, a framework with far-reaching implications. To Samuel Bowles, she wrote, "How failure in a Battle—were easier—and you here" (L 277). And to Louise and Frances Norcross, she wrote:

> Sorrow seems to me more general that it did, and not the estate of a few persons, since the war began; and if the anguish of others helped one with one's own, now would be many medicines.
> 'Tis dangerous to value, for only the precious can alarm. I noticed that Robert Browning had made another poem, and was astonished—till I remembered that I myself, in my smaller way, sang off charnel steps. [L 298]

Many of Dickinson's concerns are evident in this letter: sorrow, anguish; the dangers of attachment, since the precious can be lost at great pain; and poetry, her own and others'. These are her familiar subjects and certainly reflect her inner life and personal sensibility. In this letter, however, she places her own concerns in the context of the national trauma through which she was then living. Her anguish is reflected in the anguish of others. Her fears of loss are validated by fatalities in battle. In fact, her image of the world as an uncertain and treacherous place becomes, in the context of war, less pathological. The war magnified disorders she already sensed. Its exigencies could only have focused her fears and made them more pressing. The explosion of poetic energy that took place during the war years certainly suggests this. Dickinson's preoccupation with anguish and loss need not be seen as the product of an individual and morbid imagination. She writes here of her surprise that Browning could continue to compose poetry after his wife's death. But Dickinson also writes in the face of death and disaster. When she asserts that she "sang off charnel steps," she is only being literal.

The war seemed to her an all too potent demonstration of the incoherence, even the violence, that characterized her view of ordinary life. To Higginson, stationed in South Carolina, she wrote: "War feels to me an oblique place. . . . I found you were gone, by accident, as I find Systems are, or Seasons of the year, and obtain no cause—but suppose it a treason of Progress, that dissolves as it goes" (L 280). To someone for whom the flux of the seasons presented a painful spectacle of the transitory and the arbitrary, the violence of a fratricidal war would indeed be difficult to fathom. In one of the poems cited by Thomas Ford as a poem of war, Dickinson compares the violence of battle, not to extraordinary cataclysms, but to the usual processes of nature:

> They dropped like Flakes—
> They dropped like Stars—
> Like Petals from a Rose—
> When suddenly across the June
> A wind with fingers—goes— [P 409]

The comparison of battle to snow and wind, far from making the death of soldiers seem more natural, makes nature seem sudden and frightening. The mundane world of falling leaves and passing time was, to Dickinson, discontinuous enough. The common suffering of departure and death was sufficiently incomprehensible. With the war, Dickinson was faced with a compelling threat of unaccountable interruptions, losses, and massacres. Had the world not seemed to her a disrupted place before, it certainly would appear so after 1861.

Dickinson's poems become less idiosyncratic, more unified, and acquire broader implications once this context is admitted. Even more than in her letters, the presence of war in Dickinson's poetry has been greatly underestimated. Besides the sizable number of poems directly addressing the war, there are many more that involve martial imagery either incidentally or extensively. And still more poems indirectly reflect the martial backdrop against which they were written. Nor are these discontinuous from one another. Martial imagery is applied to situations unrelated to war. War poems present the same questions and fears Dickinson habitually treated. This argues for, rather than against, the enduring power the national trauma had on Dickinson's imagination. If the same attitudes prevail with regard to violent conflict as do with regard to her constant concerns, this suggests the degree to which violence had infused her world rather than that her sense of violence was quotidian. Thus, while in "They dropped like Flakes," nature is a figure for the violence of war, in "Whole Gulfs of Red" the violence of war is a figure for nature:

> Whole Gulfs—of Red, and Fleets—of Red—
> And Crews—of solid Blood—
> Did place about the West—Tonight—
> As 'twere specific Ground—
>
> And They—appointed Creatures—
> In Authorized Arrays—
> Due—promptly—as a Drama—
> That bows—and disappears—   [P 658]

This is one of a number of poems in which sunsets or storms are described as battles.[11] Here, the sky is compared to "specific Ground," and that ground is defined by the color of blood and by military formations. The second stanza then shifts the comparison from spatial to temporal terms. "I found you were gone, by accident, as I find Systems are, or Seasons of the year," Dickinson had written to Higginson when he went off to war. In "Whole Gulfs of Red," the sunset scene is established, only to disappear "promptly." Like men who go off to battle and do not return, the close of day presents an image of instability and dissolution. In both cases, the actors suddenly vanish. There is as well a common fatality. The combatants are "appointed," "Authorized," and "Due." The setting of the sun, the mere motion of time, involves, as does war, an irrevocable passing away. In both, participants are ordained to be annihilated. This is a traumatized view of sunset. War here serves as the model in terms of which Dickinson perceives the day's decline and which renders that decline terrible and fearful.

Wallace Stevens, in *The Necessary Angel*, describes the imagination as a "violence from within that protects us from a violence without." In Dickinson, inner violence confronted outer violence. Far from remaining detached from the civil conflagration, Dickinson internalized it. The plight of soldiers was one with which she could identify. Both she and they seemed trapped in a situation beyond their control:

> I never hear of prisons broad
> By soldiers battered down,
> But I tug childish at my bars
> Only to fall again.   [P 77]

Both she and they had to ward off unforeseen attacks. Of confronting the past, Dickinson writes:

> Unarmed if any meet her
> I charge him fly
> Her faded Ammunition
> Might yet reply.   [P 1203]

Both she and they could suddenly be overtaken by danger. Of her own loneliness, she writes:

> Did you ever look in a Cannon's face—
> Between whose Yellow eye—
> And yours—The Judgment intervened—
> The Question of 'To die'—   [P 590]

In short, both she and they lived in a world altogether unpredictable and terrifying, in which life hung by a thread:

> A Day! Help! Help! Another Day!
> Your prayers, oh Passer by!
> From such a common ball as this
> Might date a Victory!
> From marshallings as simple
> The flags of nations swang.
> Steady—my soul: What issues
> Upon thine arrow hang!   [P 42]

Dickinson was appalled at how the random shot could spare or destroy. Life in battle was dependent upon the accidental and contingent. Thus Frazer Stearns's "big heart" was "shot away by a minnie ball" (L 255). Thus one who "Bestowed Himself to Balls" and

"Invited Death—with bold attempt—" was spared, while others "Coy of Death" were killed in battle (P 759). But the poet's life was also exposed to the accidental. Day followed day, each a threat, disconnected from the other. Her own inner life depended on "marshallings," the rallying of forces within her. Although this poem was written in 1858, before the Civil War had actually commenced, the rhetoric of war and the conflict of issues were already making themselves felt in the national consciousness. That rhetoric is suggested here. And Dickinson sees her own survival as depending no less upon the "common ball," the random shot, which could change the balance of battle for actual soldiers.

In these poems, the situation faced by the soldier on the field dramatizes, and even defines, the situation Dickinson felt herself to be facing. Her inner world is described in language surprisingly violent. Anguish for her is a "Terror as consummate / As Legions of Alarm / Did leap, full flanked, upon the Host" (P 565). Personal conflict acquires military contours:

'Twas fighting for his Life he was—
That sort accomplish well—
The Ordnance of Vitality
Is frugal of its Ball.

It aims once—kills once—conquers once—
There is no second War
In that Campaign inscrutable
Of the Interior.   [P 1188]

The subject of this poem is clearly an internal experience, of which battle remains figurative. But the sense of inner crisis and, not least, of violence seems not only expressed through, but modeled on, exterior combat. The choice of combat as her figure for the poem's desperation and finality reflects Dickinson's conception of battle as much as it does her inward experience. It becomes difficult, after a certain point, to determine whether war is an image of Dickinson's inner turmoil or whether her "Campaign inscrutable" is an image of war. Each conflagration mirrors the other.

Such crossing of inward with outward violence was not exclusive to Dickinson. Robert Penn Warren describes Herman Melville's confrontation with the Civil War in similar terms: "The deep divisions of

Melville's inner life, . . . the struggle between his natural skepticisms and his yearning for religious certitude . . . now found, we may hazard, in the fact of a civil war an appropriate image." For Melville, inner questions and external events conjoined, such that "the centrifugal whirl toward violent action" finally was balanced by "the centripetal pull toward an inwardness of apparently unresolvable mystery or tormenting ambiguity" of Melville's habitual perplexity.[12]

This confluence of strifes, invoking the issues most central to the writer, is similarly suggested by Louis Martz for Walt Whitman—and for Dickinson as well. Martz sees "the external struggle of the Civil War, and the internal struggle of the poets" as deriving from the "problems of a world and a self hovering between dissolution and creation" common to both Whitman and Dickinson.[13] But Martz does not pursue the implications of this insight for Dickinson. And it is not assumed for her, as it is for both Melville and Whitman, that war penetrates her work, the pressure of events meeting her inward pressures. Melville's and Whitman's involvement is, admittedly, explicit in the poetic record each left in *Battle-Pieces* and *Drum-Taps*. Whitman even went so far as to claim, in "A Backward Glance o'er Traveled Roads," that

> although I had made a start before, only . . . from the strong flare and provocation of [the] war's sights and scenes the final reasons-for-being of an autochthonic and passionate song definitely came forth. . . . without those three or four years and the experiences they gave, Leaves of Grass would not now be existing.[14]

Emily Dickinson was never so overt. But for her, too, the war raised pressing questions, continuous with and framing her profoundest concerns.

The violence of Dickinson's inner life took on impelling form in the context of war. War dramatically confirmed the anguish and confusion that constituted her world. Death in particular had always seemed the epitome of incomprehensible sorrows and sudden blows. War intensified this image. How many poems concerned with death arose directly out of the spectacle of the war cannot be estimated.

> The only News I know
> Is Bulletins all Day
> From Immortality   [P 827]

41

can be called a war poem with certainty only because it was written in a letter to Higginson, in which Dickinson was panic-stricken after reading in the *Republican* that he had been wounded (L 290). In an 1863 letter to Higginson (L 282), Dickinson wrote:

> The possibility—to pass
> Without a Moment's Bell—
> Into Conjecture's presence—
> Is like a Face of Steel—
> That suddenly looks into ours
> With a metallic grin—
> The Cordiality of Death—
> Who drills his Welcome in—   [P 286]

The year and Higginson's place in South Carolina makes us attend to the imagery of artillery—"a Face of Steel," "a metallic grin"—which might otherwise be overlooked.

Gunfire here is Dickinson's paradigm for the suddenness of death in general. But it was not the unpredictable nature of death that most disturbed her. This might have been bearable, had she believed that death was part of a general pattern to existence and that this pattern had meaning. It was not merely random death, but insignificant death that seemed unacceptable.

The traditional consolation for death was, of course, immortality. Religion asserted that this world gave way to the next, that all that transpires here and now is part of a divine scheme leading to an afterworld. Every event is seen to have its place within, and to contribute to, this scheme. Emily Dickinson, however, found it difficult to accept this explanation. Louis Martz describes Whitman's as a prophetic voice, one that "speaks for God and interprets the divine will to man" and affirms utterance as a "divine, creative process" beyond the wounds and sickness of war. Dickinson, in contrast, lived "in doubt, in fear, in danger."[15] She was reluctant to interpret through her voice the divine will, either for the mere passing of time and the ordinary occurrence of death or for war's extreme disruption. These two levels—the ordinary and the cataclysmic—seemed to her increasingly commensurate. She integrated the violence of war with the fact of death itself. Together they formed one image of the world, an image for which religious promises remained an uncertain assurance and the divine will, mysterious:

> Some we see no more, Tenements of Wonder
> Occupy to us though perhaps to them
> Simpler are the Days than the Supposition
> Their removing Manners
> Leave us to presume
>
> That oblique Belief which we call Conjecture
> Grapples with a Theme stubborn as Sublime
> Able as the Dust to equip its feature
> Adequate as Drums
> To enlist the Tomb.   [P 1221]

The dead are seen no more, as they pass to a world about which the living continue to wonder in ignorance. Perhaps to the dead, their new state seems simple and unmysterious. But those left behind remain with only the "Supposition" that death occasions. The dead may understand their own removal. The living can only imagine and presume.

Death, then, poses a problem which cannot be resolved with any certainty—a problem, Dickinson suggests, equally arising from the "Dust" of the grave in general (which here, as able "to equip," acquires a military resonance) and from the "Drums" of war in particular. The "oblique Belief" in immortality is only "Conjecture" and finally does not assuage doubts and fears. Dickinson restates this uncertainty in an elegy for Francis Dickinson, the first Amherst war death:

> If pride shall be in Paradise—
> Ourself cannot decide—
> Of their imperial Conduct—
> No person testified—   [P 596]

A promise of paradise does not resolve the poet's doubts. As an answer, it is much less certain than the fact of death it attempts to explain.

Dickinson's faith in immortality was undermined by more than lack of evidence about the afterlife. There seemed to her inherent faults in the doctrine of an afterworld. Death was presented as an integral part of God's design; but she could not accept death into a divinely sanctioned scheme. Instead, the divine plan itself seemed suspect to her. Any death presented Dickinson with this problem:

> It's easy to invent a Life—
> God does it—every Day—
> Creation but the Gambol
> Of His Authority—
>
> It's easy to efface it—
> The thrifty Deity
> Could scarce afford Eternity
> To Spontaneity—
>
> The Perished Patterns murmur—
> But his Perturbless Plan
> Proceed—inserting Here—a Sun—
> There—leaving out a Man—   [P 724]

Emily Dickinson had been taught that God's design appoints both life and death. Both are instances of his will. But to her eyes, he effaces as willingly as he creates. There then may be some flaw in the pattern itself or in the will directing it. God's authority gambols capriciously in a near oxymoron. Yet death was not only part of his purpose, but his particular realm, his seat of judgment. To her, however, death seemed an evil without consolation. If it were part of God's design, she considered him randomly cruel. He is a "thrifty Deity" who cannot afford to alter his eternal plan in spontaneous mercy for his creatures. He willfully proceeds, "inserting Here—a Sun— / There— leaving out a Man." But Dickinson protested for each "Perished Pattern." She contested the design that effaces as easily as it invents.

Into this context, Dickinson placed the war:

> The seeing pain one can't relieve makes a demon of one. If angels have heart beneath their silver jackets, I think such things could make them weep, but Heaven is so cold! It will never look kind to me that God, who causes all, denies such little wishes. It could not hurt His glory, unless it were a lonesome kind. I 'most conclude it is. [L 234]

Dickinson did not specify what pain she had in mind. But as she also added, "When did the war really begin?" War or peace, Dickinson could not be certain of divine benevolence. And if the evil of death made her question God's "Perturbless Plan," then the great evil of war certainly could not be justified by appeal to the divine will, which, as she writes elsewhere, enters the many war dead on its "Repealless List" (P 409). Far from being comforted by faith during the war, she could only protest more strongly against the supposed design of which even war is a part. This would be the case, perhaps, regarding any catastrophe. But the Civil War in particular raised these exact questions of design and purpose. The degree to which religious justifications became suspect to Dickinson, especially with regard to war, was also due to the nature of the war itself.

The Civil War deeply implicated the whole institution of religion in America. Its outbreak was marked with a call, not only from the government, but from the churches, for the country to stand or fall. The issues at stake were universal and spiritual rather than local and political only. James Moorhead, in *American Apocalypse*, demonstrates the degree to which the approaching war was seen as the crisis in an apocalyptic drama. It was believed that good and evil would finally clash on the fields of Armageddon in an ultimate test, not only of the nation, but of the world. The Civil War was to be *the* turning point in the providential plan. To the participants, it seemed that

> God was violently overturning the old, corrupt order and was bringing the disparate forces of history to a climactic resolution in one place and time. It had been granted to Americans to fight the definitive battle that would ensure the future happiness of the nation and the world.[16]

This rehetoric of apocalypse infused the sermons of the period. Thus, one preacher told the Northampton Volunteers: "If the crusaders, seized by a common enthusiasm, exclaimed, 'It is the will of God! It is the will of God!'—much more may we make this our rallying cry and inscribe it on our banners."[17] It infused political orations, as in the speech delivered by Oliver Wendell Holmes, Sr., on the fourth of July, 1863:

> If this war is no accident, . . . if it is for no mean, unworthy end, but for national life everywhere, for humanity, for the kingdom of God on earth; if it is not hopeless, but only growing to such dimensions that the world

shall remember the final triumph of right throughout all time; . . . then the bells may ring. . . . This is our Holy War, and we must fight it against that great General who will bring to it all the powers with which he has fought against the Almighty before he was cast down from heaven.[18]

It infused the nation as a whole, as the sweeping popularity of the "Battle Hymn of the Republic" attests:

> I have read a fiery gospel writ in burnished rows
>   of steel;
> As ye deal with my contemners, so with you my grace
>   shall deal;
> Let the Hero, born of woman, crush the serpent with
>   his heel;
>
> > Since God is marching on.

In the military camps and the glint of guns, the nation believed itself to be witnessing the coming of the Lord and the Final Judgment.

The intensity with which religious rhetoric was applied to political events in the Civil War reflects a long tradition in American history. American politics had, from the outset, been profoundly imbued, if not actively fashioned, by a Puritan interpretation of Old Testament relations between the nation and God. The belief of the Puritan founders that God had elected them a chosen people, sending them on a sacred errand into the wilderness in order to erect a truly Christian society, became, with the founding of the United States, integral to the national identity. God had elected America for a special destiny among the nations. The evidence of "the time of the discovery of the American continent," "the circumstances of its colonization," its "system of popular government," its "domain and unlimited resources," all attested that "God had given us a high destiny to fill, of honor to ourselves and of good to mankind."[19] Secular and sacred history thus came to be identified in an ultimate providential design, with America, as Sacvan Bercovitch explains, "a symbol of their fusion: a federal identity not merely associated with the work of redemption, but intrinsic to the unfolding pattern . . . itself a prophecy to be fulfilled."[20]

The churches, accordingly, became active participants in the shaping of the country. Preachers adopted the Calvinist principle that obedience to God's will applied to the nation no less than to the individual.[21] From colonization onward, the genres of political and spiritual exhortation combined with each other, joining public welfare with personal welfare. At the time of new nationhood and new expansion, this became one means for unifying the different peoples and places. The role of the churches in shaping the consciousness of the first generations of Americans has been explored by Emory Elliott in *Power and the Pulpit in Puritan New England*. Perry Miller, in *The Life of the Mind in America*, has carefully traced the various needs to which the churches were responding and the various effects of church response. The very notion of patriotism became linked to the notion of Christian devotion. Not only individuals, but the community as a whole, should be consecrated to God. In this way the church helped to define the idea of community. In 1829, the *Spectator* announced that just as the Gospel can save individuals, so also "it can renew the face of communities and nations. The same heavenly influence which . . . descends on families and villages . . . may in like manner descend to refresh and beautify the whole land." As Perry Miller writes, the clergy "were not preaching nationalism, they were enacting it."[22]

In the nineteenth century, this religious/nationalist impulse took on decisive and practical form. According to Perry Miller, "the dominant theme in America from 1800 to 1860 is the invincible persistence of the revival technique."[23] Religious fervor was expressed in the massive religious revivals that recurred throughout the period, as well as in an unprecedented and intensive outburst of reform and missionary activity. National destiny was to involve the conversion and sanctification of the people, the land, and finally, the world. The impulse was essentially millennial. The nation was "destined to be the nucleus not only of a holy but of a millennial people."[24] Theirs was a redemptive role in a universal history. The goal was nothing less than the Kingdom of Christ, not only in the world to come, but in the world of nature.[25] This Kingdom was variously conceived, as were the means for achieving it. But America was surely its special instrument and supreme instance.

The churches, as the directors of reform and missionary activities, wielded enormous power and authority. They, rather than the government, were responsible for social questions. And they commanded the largest audience, reaching the public not only through schools and sermons but also through tracts and journals. There were more than three hundred religious journals in the United States by 1865. The Methodist publications alone claimed more than 400,000 subscribers. Secular newspapers regularly published sermons and religious editorials as well. The clergy were leading figures in national movements and had a powerful voice in national affairs. Church and secular history are, in this period, closely linked. And the period itself was informed with a deeply established tradition of millennial hopes of which the Civil War, in all its apocalyptic fury, was the culmination.

Once the war broke out, it was viewed as part of this millennial pattern and even as that pattern's ultimate moment. Each American writer had in turn to confront this stance, and the writings about the war reflect the various efforts to decipher, in the nation's history, a sacred text. To some, this text seemed strangely garbled. Hawthorne, in his introduction to *Our Old Home*, describes the war as a "hurricane that is sweeping us all along with it, possibly, into a limbo of which our nation and its polity may be as literally the fragments of a shattered dream as my unwritten romance." In "Chiefly about War Matters," he warns:

> No human effort, on a grand scale, has ever yet resulted according to the purpose of its projectors. The advantages are always incidental. Man's accidents are God's purposes. We miss the good we sought, and do the good we little cared for.[26]

Melville, too, could declare in *White Jacket* that, by making them believe God leads them to victory, "war almost makes blasphemers of the best of men." Or in "The Conflict of Conviction" of *Battle-Pieces*, Melville describes the war in one of his several voices, not as a fulfilled eschatology, but as "man's latter fall."

And yet, in "Chiefly about War Matters," Hawthorne could also include an editorial note (written in fact by himself) protesting that "the councils of wise and good men are often coincident with the purposes of Providence; and the present war promises to illustrate our remark." Between the text of the article and its editing,

Hawthorne inscribed his own vacillations. Similarly, in "The Conflict of Convictions," Melville's second voice could argue that the cataclysm of war furthers America's mission:

> So deep must the stones be hurled
> Whereon the throes of ages rear
> The final empire and the happier world.

Such ambivalence was, in Melville's case, founded in the conflict between a general condemnation of war and a sense that the Civil War, with its immediate political goals, had some justification.[27] Emancipation, he writes in his "Supplement" to *Battle-Pieces*, "was accomplished not by deliberate legislation; only through agonized violence could so mighty a result be effected." And it is ultimately a sense of divinely sanctioned ends as justifying military means that emerges as dominant, whatever doubts concerning means may also be registered.

This is finally true of Emerson and of Whitman as well. Emerson, who had earlier denounced war as, at best, "the first brutish effort to be men," comes instead to defend it, not only as justified, but "as necessary as . . . puberty to the human individual." "There have been revolutions which were not in the interest of feudalism and barbarism," he insists, "but in that of society."[28] The Civil War raised particular issues that reached beyond general qualms. The nation itself was threatened, not only by the war, but by its prewar development and direction. Antebellum America, with its materialism, slavery, and government no better than a "cacocracy ruled by the patrons of barrooms," seemed to Emerson to be betraying the American mission.[29] Of this America he could declare "the war, with its defeats and uncertainties is immensely better than what we lately called the integrity of the Republic." And in his Harvard commencement speech, he finally claims for the war a transcendent ordinance:

> Even Divine Providence, we may say, always seems to work after a certain military necessity. . . . The proof that war also is within the highest right, is a marked benefactor in the hands of Divine Providence, is its morale. The war gave back integrity to this erring and immoral nation.

Ultimately, it is not only providence that justifies the war but the war that justifies providence: "The war," writes Emerson, "made Divine Providence credible to many who did not believe the good Heaven quite honest."[30]

For Whitman, too, the war came to seem a necessity if America were to fulfill its mission. In *Memoranda during the War*, he writes that

> It is certain to me that the United States, by virtue of the Secession War and its results, and through that and them only, are now ready to enter, and must certainly enter, upon their genuine career in history . . . a development which could not possibly have been achiev'd on any less terms, or by any other means than that War.[31]

Whitman shared Emerson's alarm at growing American materialism and similarly saw the war as a possible remedy for it. But during the war's conduct, while Emerson emphasized abolitionism, Whitman focused on the need to save the Union. Secession raised his fears, as he writes in *Specimen Days*, lest America's "union should be broken, her future cut off, and that she should be compell'd to descend to the level of kingdoms and empires ordinarily great." At stake is America as "the result and the justifier of all."[32]

To affirm such Unionist patriotism, Whitman had first to overcome his sense of the war's horror. This can be traced through the revisions of poems later included in *Drum-Taps*, from which grotesque descriptions of the wounded are muted or omitted.[33] But he finally produced, in the published version, paeans to the war's glorious and even apocalyptic outcome:

> —What whispers are these, O lands, running ahead
>   of you, passing under the seas?
> Are all nations communing? is there going to be
>   but one heart to the globe?
> Is humanity forming, en-masse?—for lo! tyrants
>   tremble, crowns grow dim!
> The earth, restive, confronts a new era, perhaps
>   a general divine war;
> No one knows what will happen next—such portents
>   fill the days and nights.[34]

A divine war, a new humanity: the war affirms America's high mission. It is a fulfillment of prophecy, a sign for the future.

Emily Dickinson, however, did not find the appeal to a divine plan convincing. She could see little good in the war as such. And she could not be comforted by assurances of a providential scheme into which it would take its place and be validated:

My Triumph lasted till the Drums
Had left the Dead alone
And then I dropped my Victory
And chastened stole along
To where the finished Faces
Conclusion turned on me
And then I hated Glory
And wished myself were They.

What is to be is best descried
When it has also been—
Could Prospect taste of Retrospect
The tyrannies of Men
Were Tenderer—diviner
The Transitive toward.
A Bayonet's contrition
Is nothing to the Dead.   [P 1227]

The notion of predestination, of providence, had traditionally been applied to the lives of individuals. Millennialism applied it to the nation and to history as well.[35] The war was seen as part of a millennial patter, but Dickinson refused to regard it as a moment in sacred history from which point of view it would be retroactively just. She denounced suffering and death, even after victory. The second stanza at first seems to concede that "Retrospect" would render "Prospect" more tender and divine. In an image of reading not unlike that found in the "Battle Hymn," where a "Fiery gospel" is "read" in "burnished rows of Steel," Dickinson admits that "What is to be" may be "best descried / When it has also been." But this concession is then retracted. In the moment of occurrence, this is small comfort. Nor is it very relevant to the "finished Faces." The contrition of guns is, the poet concludes, "Nothing to the Dead." The future is not accessible to the present, and the pattern as a whole may finally be irrelevant.

Dickinson had ample access to the attitudes about war with which this poem obliquely argues. Throughout the years preceding the war's outbreak, millennial rhetoric had permeated the press. It penetrated Dickinson's sanctum by such seemingly innocuous infiltrators as *Harper's Monthly* and the *Springfield Republican*. *Harper's* was not a religious journal. But it printed such editorials as:

> "Providence in American History": We share the conviction that Providence has presided over the colonization and progress of this country . . . and cling to the belief that Providence has its purpose in our national growth and will fulfill its far-reaching scheme. . . . It is true now as true of old in Horeb: "Put off thy shoes from off thy feet; for the place whereon thou standest is holy ground."

> "The End and the Beginning": As time goes on every man finds himself forming definite relations with other men and with God's Providence. A nation is subject to the same law, and when we are meditating any great public issue we must consider its bearing in this light: How will it affect us as subjects of the divine kingdom, called to live under the divine law of grace?

> "Valor": True valor is that manly force that makes the Right prevail, and as such it is a pre-eminent moral and religious trait, for what is morality and religion but the spirit . . . that sets up God's kingdom among men? . . . Every true man yearns to find his authority in the highest sanctions, and when he lifts his arm in defense of his country he shudders at the bare thought of following his own will instead of that Supreme will which the Providence of God has lodged in the laws and magistrates of the nation.[36]

The Springfield Republican, too, published throughout the war years a column on "Piety and Patriotism." In it, the activities of the clergy during the war were reported and sermons were printed. One notice has particular interest with regard to Emily Dickinson. The *Republican* of 13 July 1861, printed President Stearns's Amherst College commencement sermon (annually delivered at the Dickinson home). First Stearns is quoted:

> There is progress in our land; all the forces of selfish and irresponsible power are mustering, that they may confederate and be broken. . . . We cannot always see the immediate results of any struggle; but we may be sure that God is on the side of Theism against idolatry, on the side of liberty against despotism, and in the end right must prevail.

The *Republican* reporter comments:

> It is the right of the class to . . . sustain the justice of God by upholding a free and righteous government among men. But above all things, "Stand up for Jesus." He heads the conflict and wears the crown, and His victorious soldiers will be princes. Stand firmly with him. . . You fight under the eye of your leader, and remember, "He that overcometh shall inherit all things."

The spirit and rhetoric of the period had indeed penetrated Amherst. Amherst even performed a significant role in the church activities that characterized nineteenth-century America. The college had been founded as a stronghold of Presbyterian orthodoxy to join with Andover and Princeton seminaries against the heresies of Unitarian Harvard. The college church was dedicated "to advance the kingdom of Christ the Redeemer by training many pious youths for the Gospel ministry." In his *History of Amherst College*, William Tyler writes that the college itself was founded "with express reference to a general revival of religion and the conversion of the world." The outbreak of war enlisted this ardor for the cause of the Union. Tyler makes the proud claim, "No class of men, as statistics prove, contributed to the grand army which saved the Union and the nation in the Civil War in so large proportion to their numbers . . . as the graduates and undergraduates of our college."[37]

The town's and college's commitment to the war effort is fully displayed in the many sermons and celebrations documented in *The Years and Hours of Emily Dickinson*. *The Years and Hours* further records Edward Dickinson's involvement in these occasions. It was he who organized the financing of uniforms for volunteers, presided at the ceremony of the departing enlisted men, and organized the raising of a new Amherst regiment. His own stance can also be glimpsed. In a public letter, he wrote:

> Would to Heaven! That all the American people could be aroused by what is past . . . and resolve that by the help of the Almighty God, not another inch of our soil heretofore consecrated to freedom, shall hereafter be polluted by the advancing tread of slavery.[38]

The atmosphere in Emily Dickinson's home, and in Amherst, was thus theopolitically charged. Her education was no less so. Dickinson first attended Amherst Academy, the grammar school attached to the college, then Mount Holyoke, which, like Amherst College, was founded through missionary zeal. Mount Holyoke's "brightest, most decided feature," wrote Mary Lyon, "will be that it is a school for Christ, . . . designed to cultivate the missionary spirit among its pupils." The school's routine included prayer meetings, religious revivals, sermons, exhortations to conversion, and fasts—including a fast every first Monday in January which, in accordance with a Presbyterian rule, was dedicated to the conversion of the world.[39] The call to work for the Kingdom of Christ reached Emily Dickinson as it reached the nation.

With the war's outbreak, the familiar millennial rhetoric broke its metaphorical bonds and became impellingly literal, as James Moorhead recounts:

> Millennial imagery, of course, depicts marching armies and sanguinary battles, and thus the struggle of saints, even if spiritualized, is potentially separated from more carnal warfare by a thin line only. After fighting their apocalyptic contest with saber and rifle, Northern Churchmen were in danger of losing sight of that boundary altogether.[40]

In Emily Dickinson's work, militant imagery appears in religious contexts, reflecting the rhetoric of her age. The saints and conscience she calls "martial" (P 60, 1598). Salvation is a "Victory" (P 461, 550, 984, 1072) or a "Glory" (P 296, 420, 694, 696, 1370). Such martial-religious tropes become in turn image systems. The saved are "Victors" who pass to a world where "Surrender—is a sort unknown" and "Defeat—an outgrown Anguish" (P 325). These are traditional topoi for the Church Militant.

> How many *Bullets* bearest?
> Hast Thou the Royal Scar?
> Angels! Write "Promoted"
> On this Soldier's brow!   [P 73]

Similarly may only refer to the Soldier of Christ as type.

As military imagery comes to control whole poems, however, the context in which these poems were written seems increasingly central. One poem presents the quest for salvation entirely as a struggle between victory and defeat, declaring in its conclusion:

> And if I gain! Oh Gun at Sea!
> Oh Bells, that in the Steeples be!
> At first, repeat it slow!   [P 172]

Another poem presents death as "the waning lamp / That lit the Drummer from the Camp" (P 259). Images grow more concrete, more specific. Details accrue. The war imagery comes to be drawn with a precision that suggests an actual model.

Dickinson's poems—whether written in the years immediately preceding the war, when the volume of millennial and martial religious rhetoric was increasing, or written during the war's progress, as most in fact were, or written in the war's aftermath—invoke battle certainly, in part, as a type for the inner struggle of the soul. But there are poems that undoubtedly suggest that some outward battle is before the poet if only as a foil to the traditional imagery in which soul and angels are soldiers of God:

> To fight aloud is very brave—
> But gallanter, I know
> Who charge within the bosom
> The Cavalry of Woe—
>
> Who win, and nations do not see—
> Who fall—and none observe—
> Whose dying eyes, no Country
> Regards with patriot love—
>
> We trust, in plumed procession
> For such, the Angels go—
> Rank after Rank, with even feet—
> And Uniforms of Snow.   [P 126]

Here, as elsewhere, combat penetrates Dickinson's private world. In this inner sense, every civilian is a soldier, and every soldier fights an inward war. Dickinson as poet had little interest in the specific facts of military strategy. But the battle which "no Country / Regards with patriot love" is in pointed contrast with the battle patriotism recognizes. Dickinson sees her inward strife as like the strife of objective battlefields. Her imagination makes her own world in the image of the world of war.

It also projects her into battle, where she could identify with soldiers, no longer as types only, but in the flesh:

My Portion is Defeat—today—
A paler luck than Victory—
Less Paeans—fewer Bells—
The Drums don't follow Me—with tunes—
Defeat—a somewhat slower—means—
More Arduous than Balls—

'Tis populous with Bone and stain—
And Men too straight to stoop again,
And Piles of solid Moan—
And Chips of Blank—in Boyish Eyes—
And scraps of Prayer—
And Death's surprise,
Stamped visible—in Stone—

There's somewhat prouder, over there—
The Trumpets tell it to the Air—
How different Victory
To Him who has it—and the One
Who to have had it, would have been
Contenteder—to die—   [P 639]

This poem does not entirely exclude the metaphoric level. A defeat "More Arduous than Balls" may be an inward one. It may be, however, a defeat as worse than death, as the end of the poem suggests. It is easier to die if victorious. But whether the poem finally addresses an internal or an external state, it is certainly situated in the external world. The second stanza could not be more concrete. Like Clytemnestra imagining herself at Troy in Aeschylus' *Agamemnon*, the poet is on the battlefield, observing and recording a density of details: bone and stain, corpses and moans, trumpets and drums. "Death's surprise" is stamped visible. "Scraps of Prayer" is a literal image as well. Dickinson here is not using the rhetoric of martial religion. She is stating a fact. To Higginson, she wrote, "I trust you may pass the limit of War, and though not reared to prayer—when service is had in

Church, for our Arms, I include yourself" (L 280). In the Holy Crusade of the Civil War, prayers were included in the arsenal.

Church involvement in the war effort began at home, with prayers of civilians and with exhortations to enlist. Sermons proclaimed that "God is treading the wine press alone . . . for the day of vengeance is in His heart, and the year of His redeemed is come." To fight was a Christian duty. The volunteers heard the same message after their arrival in the military camps. Giant prayer meetings were held in the field. The army was seen as a "vast chapel," of which one minister wrote, "Probably no army, in any age, has ever witnessed such out-pourings of the Spirit of God as our own armies have experienced." Contemporary estimates range from 100,000 to 200,000 conversions among the soldiers.[41] In 1864 alone, the Christian Commission distributed 6 million books such as Newman Hall's *Come to Jesus*, 1 million hymnals and books of psalms, 1 million Bibles, and 11 million tracts.[42]

American soldiers died with prayers on their lips, quite literally. Moreover, they did so on both sides. Both North and South had received the tradition of a special destiny for a chosen people. If, in the South, this acquired a utopian rather than an apocalyptic character,[43] the war nevertheless inspired the South with a millennial fervor equal to that in the North. Each side saw itself as the incarnation of Good battling against the Antichrist. Each side claimed divine sanction for its cause. Leonidas Polk, the Episcopal bishop of Louisiana, declared his most solemn belief "that it is for constitutional liberty, which seems to have fled to us for refuge, for our hearth stones and our altars that we strike." Thomas March Clark, the Episcopal bishop of Rhode Island, preached to a departing militia: "It is a holy and righteous cause in which you enlist. . . . God is with us. The Lord of Hosts is on our side.[44] Soldiers, both North and South, went to war with the same devotion and the same faith.

This state of affairs did not escape notice. Hawthorne, in a letter to Francis Bennoch, reports that all the soldiers "are thoroughly in earnest, all pray for the blessing of heaven," and concludes, "The appeals are so numerous, fervent, and yet contradictory, that the Great Arbiter must be sorely puzzled."[45] Melville, in "Slain Collegians" of *Battle-Pieces*, recounts how from both North and South soldiers "went forth with blessings given / By Priests and Mothers in the name of heaven" only to "lie down on a midway bloody bed." In his concluding "Meditation," he christens the conflict a "Christian war of natural brotherhood." Lincoln himself was deeply troubled by mutual and contradictory invocations of heaven:

> In great contests each party claims to act in accordance with the will of God. Both may be, and one must be, wrong. God cannot be for and against the same thing at the same time. . . . By his mere great power on the minds of the now contestants, he could have either saved or destroyed the Union without a human contest. Yet the contest began. And, having begun, he could give the final victory to either side any day. Yet the contest proceeds.[46]

The Civil War combined the cataclysm of fratricide with the upheaval of a religious schism. The churches, which John C. Calhoun in 1850 in his last Senate speech had named among the strongest of "the cords that bind the states together," became instead active instruments in their dissolution. It has even been argued that "the split between the churches was not only the first break between the sections, but the chief cause of the final break."[47] Political justifications implied and invoked metaphysical ones. The American self-conception as mankind's hope for an edenic existence had helped impel the nation into war. The war itself then emerged as a great test of these American assumptions, demanding its own justifications. But in light of the double contradictory claims of North and South, this became increasingly problematic. The whole question of religious authority and sanction was inevitably raised. Spokesmen for God pronounced contradictory messages. Confidence in them could be easily shaken. The inscrutable nature of the divine will could not but obtrude. In his second inaugural address, Lincoln noted that "both [sides] read the same Bible, and pray to the same God; and each invokes his aid against the other. . . . The prayers of both could not be answered." Lincoln could, nevertheless, dedicate himself in the faith that "the Judgments of the Lord are true and righteous altogether." He could overcome his sense of the profound contradiction of the same churches invoking the same theology against each other.

This Emily Dickinson could not do. In "My Portion is Defeat" and every other war poem, she scrupulously refrained from taking sides.

She sympathized with the defeated without partisanship. She could not celebrate victory, regardless of the victors. Nor could she fathom the spectacle in which, as Lincoln stated, both sides "claim to act in accordance with God's will." She saw how "Chips of Blank" took their place with unanswered prayers in "Boyish Eyes." These prayers were "Scraps." Not only the soldiers, but the beliefs that had inspired them, were to Dickinson casualties of battle.

To Dickinson, no faith that "the Judgments of the Lord are true and righteous altogether" could redeem a war both fratricidal and schismatic. That the carnage had been ordained seemed to her small consolation. It, instead, raised questions concerning the role of providence itself. Assertions that God had willed the conflagration, or that events could be explained by an encompassing design, met in her with skepticism. She could see little good in the war as such; and she could not be comforted by assurances that it had been appointed by a providential scheme. "To interrupt His Yellow Plan," she writes, "the Sun does not allow," in a figure for God's impassible "Majesty." But she dismisses this as an indifference which "emits a Thunder" in order, unsuccessfully, "A Bomb—to justify" (P 591). Her appeals to God thus question rather than proclaim his intentions. They are not invocations, but injunctions:

> At least—to pray—is left—is left—
> Oh Jesus—in the Air—
> I know not which thy chamber is—
> I'm knocking—everywhere—
>
> Thou settest Earthquake in the South—
> And Maelstrom, in the Sea—
> Say, Jesus Christ of Nazareth—
> Hast thou no Arm for Me?   [P 502]

This poem, so characteristic of Dickinsonian prayer, stakes appeal against despair without resolution. Jesus "in the Air" is asserted, but the possibility of reaching him there is doubtful. The frantic knocking goes unanswered, in spite of the promises in Matthew 7:7. Dickinson's final "Hast thou no Arm for me?" may be a sincere plea; or it may be an accusation of neglect. Set in a stanza that invokes divine power, the hope of support perhaps outweighs the doubt of response. But Christ

as Lord of earthquake and storm is not the most approachable Deity—particularly if "the South" of the poem is more than figurative.

Richard Sewall, in his *Life* of Dickinson, cites the 1862 commencement ceremonies at Amherst as the probable source of this poem's
imagery. The day's speeches had a decided military thrust. Otis Phil-
lips Lord, whose importance to Dickinson's emotional life seems relatively well-documented, spoke of the country as a "light to nations"
and of the civic duty to prosecute the war. Henry Ward Beecher put
aside all literary discussion in deference to "public questions" which
"must take precedence," choosing instead to treat of "the questions of
the hour which are passing through a storm and an earthquake: the
storm in the North, and the earthquake in the South."[48] In terms of
Beecher's oration, the image of Christ as setting "Earthquake in the
South" grows especially ominous. It suggests Christ himself to be
directly implicated in the country's strife. And the poem as a whole
seems further to suggest that Christ's power can be felt more in
historical catastrophe than as a source of private strength. His
maelstrom is palpable. But when the poet bids him speak, no answer
seems forthcoming, except perhaps that heard in such destructive
forces.

Nothing in this poem explicitly distinguishes it as concerned with
the Civil War. Although the poem may reflect, as Sewall points out,
the memorial to Frazar Stearns, the urgings to prayer for the Union
which took place that commencement day, or the possibility that
Austin might be drafted, none of these is specified. And this, like the
poem's ambivalent appeal to God, is characteristic of Dickinson. She
concerns herself not with an overtly named occasion but rather with
metaphysical issues she feels to have been raised by them. Unlike
other northern writers, Dickinson does not address the specific issues
of slavery or of union involved in the war's politics. Nor does she cast
explanations for the war in specifically political terms. Melville might
cite the contradictions entailed in the Union as "the world's fairest
hope" linked with slavery as "man's foulest crime" ("Misgivings").
But to Dickinson the political causes are secondary to the metaphysical constructions they imply. For her, the war is war as such. What
concerns her are the metaphysical issues raised by the war and implicit in its theological rhetoric.

Dickinson's poem is therefore strangely situated between its own universality and the unavoidable but barely hinted fact of the war raging in the background of its composition. In that suppressed context, however, the ambivalent treatment of Jesus in "At least to pray" which emerges, independent of historical specificity, gains greater force and resonance. Dickinson here does not deny divine power. But she asserts it only in its aspect of unleashing catastrophe. As a force responding to human need or strengthening human weakness it remains much less certain. That contrast controls the poem. Jesus, for all his might, leaves those who appeal to him helpless. God destroys and then fails to sustain those who must confront the destruction.

Divine power in its destructive aspect became Dickinson's increasing concern. The reality of evil impressed itself upon her. And it seemed to her that actual death and suffering overwhelmed consolations regarding their possible recompense. Promised rewards, and the scheme that assumes future bliss to assuage present misery, came to seem inadequate, if not scornful:

> Victory comes late—
> And is held low to freezing lips—
> Too rapt with frost
> To take it—
> How sweet it would have tasted—
> Just a Drop—
> Was God so economical?
> His Table's spread too high for Us—
> Unless We dine on tiptoe—
> Crumbs—fit such little mouths—
> Cherries—suit Robins—
> The Eagle's Golden Breakfast strangles—Them—
> God keep His Oath to Sparrows—
> Who of little Love—know how to starve—   [P 690]

Written in 1862, and presumably commemorating the death of Frazar Stearns (L 257), this poem nevertheless evades specificities. Its opening image of victory delayed and especially of freezing corpses makes its war context clear. But Dickinson then immediately pursues her own primary interest. The political and historical spheres give way to the pressing metaphysical enigmas raised by them. The Gospels assure that not a sparrow shall fall to the ground without the Father; and religion pledges that all who have faith shall feast at Christ's table. These images of providential concern and of grace become, here, images of a God who will not use his power to redeem and whose promised glory only taunts mankind. A miserly God, he grants victory—so easy a boon—only when it can no longer save. And just as victory is ill-timed, so the saints' feast is ill-placed. Spread above the natural world, it merely tantalizes. Its "Golden Breakfast" is as unsuited to human needs as an eagle's fare would be to the needs of robins. The few crumbs that would satisfy are denied; and the pledge to sparrows of divine concern becomes here an oath un-fulfilled, a willful withholding of God's bounty, so that his creatures starve.

The poem, then, moves from a concern with military to a concern with theological victory, and the latter subsumes the former. Not Newbern, where Frazar Stearns was killed, but the whole structure of divine/human interchange is the poem's subject. Still, the victory denied in combat is made the figure for every sustenance denied God's creatures. Divine failure to redeem in battle comes to represent its failure to relieve all human trouble. The war may not have caused Dickinson's doubts concerning providential care. But it became an arena for her confrontation with the apparent divergence between a posited divine order in events and the experience of those events as disordered and painful.

Daniel Aaron, in a supplement to *The Unwritten War*, notes that to Dickinson the war was "Murder" and that it "aggravated doubts and terrors."[49] Richard Rust includes her among the "Doubters" in his anthology of responses to the Civil War.[50] But Dickinson's doubts diverge from those of other northern writers. Emerson, Whitman, Hawthorne, and Melville were all concerned, as was Dickinson, with the theological implications of political events. All responded to the nation's own attempt to read its history as a sacred text in which a special providence governs even catastrophe. And all struggled with the contradictions between the presumed metaphysical patterns and the actual events taking place. To Dickinson, however, the contradic-tions outweighed all other concerns and ultimately undermined not only a theological interpretation of political reality but the theological patterns themselves.

Sacvan Bercovitch describes how, when faced with conflicts between history and their ideal conception of it, the first generations of Americans "had no choice but to explain history away" and did no "by asserting the priority of prophecy over appearances."[51] Dickinson proceeds in the contrary direction. Not even Melville, who questions whether the events of war indeed confirm a divine plan, comes to question the divine plan itself—at least, not in *Battle-Pieces*. This Dickinson does do. Rather than interpreting actual events in terms of a divine ordinance, Dickinson comes to measure the divine scheme by actual events. The result is profound misgiving regarding the metaphysical order itself.

Dickinson's concern, therefore, was primarily metaphysical. But this did not necessitate that her vision be ahistorical. The turmoil of events that claimed to be made in a universal pattern led her, not to project providential schemata onto historical events, but to question such eternal patterns in the name of history. Millennial expectations contributed to the outbreak of the Civil War, which itself then came to present, for Dickinson, a challenge to those expectations. Men were called to die for a just cause, sanctioned by heaven. But so much death called into question both the justice of the cause and its sanction. For Dickinson, political events neither fulfilled nor validated theological patterns. Instead, events became for her a trial and test of the patterns' validity. In "Victory comes late," specific historical sorrow becomes general metaphysical accusation. Dickinson's poetry of war, as does her poetry in general, challenges metaphysical designs and does so by way of temporal considerations. She finally went beyond questioning theological interpretations of politics. She questioned theology as such in the name of the reality that she held not to be measured by the eternal world, but to be its measure.

Three

War as Theodicean Problem

> The question of the purpose of human life has been raised countless times; it has never yet received a satisfactory answer, and perhaps does not admit of one. Some of those who have asked it have added that if it should turn out that life has no purpose, it would lose all value for them. But this threat alters nothing.
> —Sigmund Freud, *Civilization and Its Discontents*

A pervasive structure in Dickinson's work is that which balances gain against loss. Repeatedly, Dickinson measures the one against the other, attempting to determine whether the privation, sorrow, and death inherent in the temporal process give rise to some positive condition. She asks whether undeniable loss can be construed as gain and, if there is some gain in and through loss, whether this vindicates anguish. The problem of suffering and its possible justification is consistently addressed, as the poet considers the various possible relations between negative and positive experiences.

At times, Dickinson does assert that there is some gain in loss, that deprivation leads to discovery. "We buy with contrast—Pang is good" (P 1133), she writes. The day is "Fairer through Fading" (P 938); the dead are seen "clearer for the Grave" (P 1666). Man's condition, in which suffering has an inevitable place, is thereby strengthened:

A Plated Life—diversified
With Gold and Silver Pain
To prove the presence of the Ore
In Particles—'tis when

A Value struggle—it exist—
A Power—will pröclaim
Although Annihilation pile
Whole Chaoses on Him—   [P 806]

Life is "diversified" by its gold and silver mixture of experiences; and, in contributing to this diversity, pain enriches. Value emerges through struggle. The poet sees this as affirming man's capacity to face annihilation, as he answers it by proclaiming his own power. And although the poem ends with chaos, it does so in at least an attempt to establish chaos as an instrument of glory.

In this poem, pain seems justified for the "Gold and Silver" diversity with which it endows life. In other poems, however, pain's compensations are less certain and its status more problematic. "We see Comparatively," the poet admits. We know the "towering high" in opposition to the low. Without such opposition, distinctions, and therefore definitions, could not be drawn. The issue seems epistemological. Contrast is essential to understanding. For Dickinson, however, there are inevitable theological implications to the epistemological problem. She continues:

> Perhaps 'tis kindly—done us—
> The Anguish—and the loss—
> The wrenching—for His Firmament
> The Thing belonged to us—   [P 534]

Loss is not simply integral to the structure of experience, nor is its purpose primarily heuristic. It can be referred to the divine will. Evil, too, is an instrument of love, ultimately furthering the divine purpose. But to Dickinson, it seems that God takes away whatever we have, appropriates it into the mysterious "Firmament" where he is supposed to dwell. The possible kindness this may entail is far less impressive than its palpable cruelty. To the poet, the divine purpose remains obscure and its activities dubious.

The justification of loss by gain, of evil by good, is essentially a theodicean structure. Positive effects justify not only negative experiences but the Author of a world in which negative experiences are so prominent. And without such justification, formidable doubt is cast upon the Author and creator of all. Divine power or divine goodness or both can be called into question. This problem of evil and suffering in a world created by a presumably omnipotent and benevolent God was succinctly formulated by Epicurus:

God either wishes to take away evils, and is unable; or He is able, and is unwilling; or He is neither willing nor able, or He is both willing and able. If He is willing and is unable, He is feeble, which is not in accordance with the character of God; if He is able and unwilling, He is envious, which is equally at variance with God; if He is neither willing nor able, He is both envious and feeble, and therefore not God; if He is both willing and able, which alone is suitable to God, from what source then are evils? or why does He not remove them?[1]

Dickinson's poetry repeatedly returns to this problem. Her preoccupation with pain and with death centers in it, and her interpretation of her world is finally dependent upon her ability to resolve the seeming contradiction between the ways of God and his presumed nature.

To do so would involve for Dickinson asserting a redemption in which good comes out of evil, thus assigning to evil a place in the redemptive pattern. This would be to follow the pattern of Christian theodicy. *"O certe necessarium Adae peccatum, quod Christi morte deletum est! O felix culpa, quae talem ac tantum meruit habere redemptorem!"* declares the *Exultet* of Easter Even. Adam's sin is not only fortunate but in some sense a precondition for the Incarnation. And the ultimate redemption in Christ emerged out of the humiliation and agony of the Passion. As A. O. Lovejoy observes, the Crucifixion was "necessary to the very possibility of the redemptive act, which . . . [is] itself a necessary, and the central, event in the divine plan of terrestrial history."[2] Milton's Adam accordingly, if somewhat daringly, proclaims:

> O Goodness infinite, Goodness immense,
> That all this good of evil shall produce,
> And evil turn to good—more wonderful
> Than that which by creation first brought forth
> Light out of darkness! Full of doubt I stand,
> Whether I should repent me now of sin
> By me done and occasioned, or rejoice
> Much more that much more good thereof shall spring—[3]

This paradox of sin and suffering as the ground for redemption in Christ forms the pattern of Christian theodicy, in which ultimate

66

salvation justifies not only the suffering of this world, but the world's Author.[4]

Emily Dickinson's poetry, however, presents a radical criticism of this structure. She is disturbed that evil should have any place whatever in a benevolent pattern, that the attainment of good should presuppose and proceed a posteriori from the experience of evil. Her criticism is directed toward the experience of suffering at every level and questions its justification even by so great a good as salvation itself:

A Tooth upon Our Peace
The Peace cannot deface—
Then Wherefore be the Tooth?
To vitalize the Grace—

The Heaven hath a Hell—
Itself to signalize—
And every sign before the Place
Is Gilt with sacrifice—   [P 459]

The "Tooth" of suffering should not lessen our peace, for it leads to the peace of sanctification by God. Grace justifies suffering, and its purpose is "to vitalize the Grace." But Dickinson suggests that the journey through sorrow to redemption may be an unnecessary peripety. Its value eludes her, and its reward does not outweigh the rigors demanded for it—rigors that seem superfluous. "Far from Love the Heavenly Father / Leads the Chosen Child," she writes, but must the pathway to heaven be "through Realm of Briar?" (P 1021). The whole need for sacrifice of any kind seemed questionable. What results, in Dickinson, is not an affirmation of grace as suffering's compensation but doubts regarding grace itself. Sacrifice is not a sign of redemption. Redemption, instead, is stained by its basis in sorrow. The very image of heaven becomes not bliss, but hell.

To Dickinson, the ultimate sorrow challenging theodicy was death. It was the final loss and the most impenetrable mystery. That death had its place in a redemptive pattern seemed unclear. And even if it had such a place, why the redemptive pattern need entail death remained a pressing question. On learning that an aunt had died,

67

Dickinson wrote to Louise Norcross: "I wish 'twas plainer, the anguish of this world. I wish one could be sure the suffering had a loving side" (L 263). Death challenged theodicy, but also made it more impelling. Without redemptive love, Dickinson's universe threatened to collapse into an inexplicable and cruel chaos.

With the Civil War, such collapse seemed imminent. The war broadened the problem of theodicy beyond the question of consolation for personal sorrow to embrace the whole order of existence. "It feels a shame to be Alive / When Men so brave are dead," Dickinson writes, and asks,

> Are we that wait—sufficient worth—
> That such Enormous Pearl
> As life—dissolved be—for Us—
> In Battle's—horrid Bowl?   [P 444]

Men were going to war and dying in battle. The spectacle only intensified Dickinson's need to justify sorrow and her difficulties in doing so.

In this, Dickinson was not alone. George Fredrickson considers the confrontation with suffering to be one of the central aspects of the Civil War experience. In *The Inner Civil War*, he writes that it was only as the war progressed "that the full horror of the struggle was brought home to the people of the North." The carnage of Shiloh, Antietam, and Fredricksburg occurred on a scale previously unknown in America, and some stance toward it became imperative:

> Such large-scale suffering was a new experience for Americans, and the
> intellectuals who favored a fierce war were faced with the seemingly
> difficult task of justifying and explaining this colossal bloodletting.

This task, however, was met by a general "willingness to live resignedly in a sea of blood and tears," deriving above all in the "conviction that the present agony was willed by God."[5] The war was justified as promoting the heavenly cause. And the justifications went further. Bloodshed and suffering were explained not only as inevitable to the war's conduct, but as necessary within the divine plan as sacrificial offerings. The war was conceived, beyond promoting particular ends, as itself a means of purgation. It was thus more than providential: it was penitential and soteriological.

This view was adopted in the North especially. The destruction came to be seen there as a direct expression of divine disapproval for the sin of slavery, which had not been sufficiently protested. Yet the collapse of the Union did not mean that God had abandoned his chosen people. He was only chastising them for failing to fulfill the mission appointed to them, especially for their "failure to stand up before the nations of the earth as a model nation, to exhibit to them the beauty and glory of free institutions."[6] With this belief, the anxiety caused by the rebellion could be assuaged. R. L. Stanton, writing in 1864, describes how "when foul treason plotted the overthrow of the Government, the hearts of many failed them. They were led to think they had wholly misinterpreted the purposes of God." But, he continues, soon the conviction was regained that the war was but

> the scourge of God for our great iniquities . . . God's ultimate design was our purification and preservation, and that to this end He would in His own way terminate the institution which had been seized upon as the occasion of our strife, and that when this were accomplished the nation would emerge from this furnace and be prepared for a higher career than were otherwise possible.[7]

This reading of history as redemptive travail, whereby the nation would be purified and reborn, perhaps found its most succinct expression in the words of John Brown: "Without the shedding of blood, there is no remission of sins."

That Emerson in turn embraced John Brown as a "new saint," declaring that his execution would "make the gallows glorious like the cross," suggests the hold of such soteriological interpretations on the American imagination.[8] Emerson's apotheosis of Brown was based on a sense that he, acting in obedience to his "inner voice," would provide the country with a "new breath" like unto "the trumpet of resurrection."[9] And if Hawthorne in turn derided Brown, declaring that "nobody was ever so justly hanged," he was almost unique in doing so.[10] At issue was the impulse to martyrology. Whitman and Melville, it is true, were relatively restrained regarding Brown. Of the execution, Whitman told Traubel: "I am never convinced by the formal martyrdoms alone; I see martyrdoms wherever I go."[11] And to Melville, he is "Weird John Brown" who stands as a

"Portent" pointing only to "The meteor of the war" while all else remained indecipherable. But such restraint gives way before the image of the assassinated Lincoln. "The tragic splendour of his death," writes Whitman in *Specimen Days*, "purging, illuminating all, throws round his form, his head, an aureole that will remain and will grow brighter through time." Melville's Lincoln emerges in *Battle-Pieces* as a "Martyr" and saint in Christ's image:

Good Friday was the day
   Of the prodigy and crime.
When they killed him in his pity,
   When they killed him in his prime
Of clemency and calm—
   When with yearning he was filled
   To redeem the evil-willed,
And though conqueror, be kind.

That the author of *Pierre* and *The Confidence Man* should write verse of martial-religious enthusiasm seems improbable. Indeed Melville's stance in *Battle-Pieces* is complicated by his unresolved ambivalence toward the soteriological figures he invokes. In his preface, he in fact duly warns that the volume contains "moods variable—and at times widely at variance." But such makings of Lincoln into a "kind of martyred Messiah," as Edmund Wilson sardonically describes it, represented an impulse general to the nation.[12] Lincoln was seen as a "bloody sacrifice upon the altar of freedom." The fact that the shooting took place on Good Friday was not overlooked. Gilbert Haven, in a national sermon, urged:

Let not the 15th of April be considered the day of his death, but let Good Friday be its anniversary. . . . We should make it a moveable fast and ever keep it beside the cross and grave of our blessed Lord, in whose service and for whose gospel he became a victim and a martyr.[13]

But if Lincoln was the ultimate, he was not the sole blood sacrifice. The whole North had undergone just such a penitential and expiatory act. Lincoln was but a further "crowning offering" of those who had "already poured out such rivers of blood in expiation of its guilty acquiescence in wrong."[14] Lincoln may have been the final sacrifice;

but the war as a whole was considered a crucible and travail necessary to American salvation.

What finally emerges is an image of the war not only as a judgment, but as a passion. This is indeed the image given to the war in Whitman's "Chanting the Square Deific," which George Fredrickson cites as Whitman's final word on the war.[15] There, Christ emerges as the prophetic voice and ascendant power over the forces of wrath and evil unleashed by the Civil War. But Christ, here, is not a militant figure. He is, rather, presented in his aspect of humbling himself and accepting death, in order to redeem the world:

All sorrow, labor, suffering, I, tallying it, absorb in myself.
Many times have I been rejected, taunted, put in prison, and
    crucified—and many times shall be again;
All the world have I given up for my dear brothers' and sisters'
    sake—for the soul's sake; . . .
(Conqueror yet—for before me all the armies and soldiers of the
    earth shall yet bow—and all the weapons of war become
    impotent:)
With indulgent words, as to children—with fresh and sane words,
    mine only;
Young and strong I pass, knowing well I am destin'd myself to an
    early death:
But my Charity has no death—my Wisdom dies not, neither early nor
    late,
And my sweet Love, bequeath'd here and elsewhere, never dies.[16]

Not military triumph, but humility and renunciation are asserted here. True victory comes through rejection, imprisonment, and crucifixion. What is urged is the suffering necessary to rebirth, the self-abnegation that redeems the self. Within this framework, sacrifice itself becomes a salvific force. Christ's passion emerges as the war's figure, bestowing upon it the force of purgation. Its deaths are sanctified; its suffering is a travail that must be passed through to attain redemption.

Dickinson, in attempting to make sense of the war, at times adopts the rhetoric and reasoning of her period. In "It feels a shame to be Alive," she declares that beyond any "Reknown" attainable by the living, the dead stand as "unsustained—Saviors" who "present Divinity" (P 444). But such glory achieves strange twists, even in affirmative poems. Melville had insisted, at least at times, "There must be other, nobler worlds for them / Who nobly yield their lives in this." The afterworld also offers consolation to Dickinson at times. The dead, she writes, arrive where

> Surrender—is a sort unknown—
> On this superior soil—
> Defeat—an outgrown Anguish—   [P 325]

Once beyond mortality,

> They cannot take me—any more
> Dungeons can call—and Guns implore
> Unmeaning—now—to me—   [P 277]

Death here is a kind of release. But, strangely, it is not so much a reward for noble earthly sacrifice as an escape from a dreadful temporal condition. And battle remains a figure for all the dangers and agonies men would want to escape.

These poems thus qualify praise of heaven with censure of earth. Dickinson treats death less as justification than as indictment and war as a type of life's ills. The image of an afterworld comes not as a recompense of war's conflicts. Rather, conflict becomes an image of Dickinson's inner strife concerning an afterworld. The angel of death appears in military dress:

> Dying! To be afraid of thee
> One must to thine Artillery
> Have left exposed a Friend—

In the mystery of a "Dying eye" the poet perceives her own most sustained confrontation: the stern fight between "Two Armies, Love and Certainty / And Love and the Reverse" (P 831). Battle signifies not glory but the confrontation between a certainty of love's conquest of death and a radical doubt as to its victory.

Dickinson, in this, is challenging a profound impulse in her American theological tradition. The notion that suffering is a central—even indispensable—element in attaining to good had been a powerful element in the self-consciousness of American nationhood. Sacvan

Bercovitch, in the *American Jeremiad,* traces the development and force of a prophetic rhetoric in the American world. A rhetoric of suffering formed a fundamental mode of American social/religious discourse. For the founding Puritan elect, tribulation only pointed to "regeneration through suffering." Divine wrath itself was an act of love.[17]

Chastisement and concern as inextricably entwined then emerged in the work of Jonathan Edwards. Edwards's millennial vision of religious revival insisted on the "noise and tumult, confusion and uproar, and darkness mixed with light, and evil with good" to be expected "in the beginning of something extraordinary and glorious." His was a time of "great outward calamities" and of "spiritual calamities and miseries." But there is, he knows from Scripture, ever "a great prevalence of infidelity just before Christ's coming to avenge his suffering church." And the church's suffering is far from indifferent:

> When Christ is mystically born into the word, to rule over all nations, it is represented . . . as being in consequence of the church's crying, and travailing in birth, and being pained to be delivered. . . . God seems now, at this very time, to be waiting for this from us. When God is about to bestow some great blessing on his church, it is often his manner . . . so to order things in his providence as to show his church their great need of it, and to bring them into distress for want of it.[18]

Edwards, as Bercovitch insists, incorporated the earlier Puritan concern for trial and tribulation into his millenarianism. In doing so, Edwards was working within the American impulse toward forging national myths out of universal patterns, as Bercovitch shows.[19] The events of the Great Awakening were seen as temporal embodiments of the eternal pattern of travail and rebirth. Ultimately, the typology of the Civil War derived as well in this characteristic American tendency to concretize such general theological structures and give to them historical specificity.

Emily Dickinson's understanding of the place of suffering for man and in history derived from such theological structures no less. The Calvinism which Amherst College had been founded to defend gave rigorous definition to the origin, operation, and end of evil. Like Augustine, for whom "all evil is either sin or punishment of sin,"[20] Calvin declared that evil entered the world with the fall of man, that it is not only a product but a penalty for sin, and that evil, beyond expressing in these ways divine justice, also expresses divine majesty and goodness. God not only punishes evil with evil. He uses evil for his own purposes, turning sin toward the great good end of salvation in Christ. Affliction becomes part of God's special providence. "The afflictions which conform us to Christ have been appointed," Calvin writes.[21] The members of the Church "must expect to be subject to a more rigid discipline under the Providence of God." Suffering offers a "consolation . . . by reminding of God's watchful Providence over the human race."[22]

Even the notion of predestination, derived from Augustine and accentuated by Calvin toward a further emphasis of divine sovereignty, affirms the ultimate glory of redemption. Augustine had written:

> For God would never have created any, I do not say angel, but even man, whose future wickedness he foreknew, unless he had equally known to what uses in behalf of the good he could turn him. . . . God judged it better to bring good out of evil than to suffer no evil to exist.[23]

Calvin's doctrine of reprobation, in asserting that God's eternal decree consigns Adam's descendents either to a just perdition or, through no merit of their own, to a merciful salvation, emphasizes God's omnipotent mercy to the elect whom he had mysteriously spared. What is involved above all is "God's mercy, gratuitous mercy, to be received, not questioned, whatever the logical implications of reprobation may seem to be to the finite, sinful reason."[24] The evil of sin and eternal damnation comes to affirm divine grandeur and mercy.

This Calvinist theology emerges in force in the writings of Jonathan Edwards, whose defense of Original Sin, predestination, and divine sovereignty leads him inevitably to the theodicean questions addressed by Augustine and Calvin before him. If God disposes all things, then he must also dispose of evil events. This Edwards asserts, but continues to insist on the perfection of divine benevolence in doing so. "It may be His pleasure so to order things that, He permitting, sin will come to pass," Edwards writes. But this is so only "for the sake of the great good that by His disposal shall be the conse-

74

quence." Edwards's argument even carries him to the point of attesting, beyond the justification of evil, its necessity:

> There is no inconsistence in supposing that God may hate a thing as it is in itself, and considered simply as evil, and yet that it may be his Will it should come to pass, considering all consequences. I believe, there is no person of good understanding, who will venture to say, he is certain that it is impossible it should be best, taking in the whole compass and extent of existence, and all consequences in the endless series of events, that there should be such a thing as moral evil in the world.[25]

The necessity of moral evil could be argued, above all, as a prerequisite to a true doctrine of redemption. The very power of Christ's redemption entails that man be in a state of sin, of "deserved destruction," "calamity," and "evil" from which he is then saved. "God would have esteemed it needless to give his Son to die for man unless there had been a prior impossibility of their having righteousness."[26] Only in the context of sin does Christ's sacrifice gain full force, and sin itself attains its proper place in the divine scheme only in the context of redemption.

In an Amherst where "Jonathan Edwards was still the rule of life"[27] Emily Dickinson had been well instructed in the doctrines of reprobation and divine sovereignty. In this theology Dickinson had been schooled, from learning her letters in *The New England Primer* with its opening rhyme—"In Adam's Fall, We sinned all"—to John Marsh's *Epitome of General Ecclesiastical History*, a required text at Mount Holyoke:

> God hath chosen a certain number of the fallen race of Adam, in Christ before the foundation of the world, unto eternal glory. . . . the rest of mankind he was pleased to pass by, and ordain to dishonor and wrath, for their sins, to the praise of his vindictive justice.[28]

Sin, she was taught, even for the reprobate, bespoke the glory of divine justice and the mercy of divine grace. Traces of these doctrines can be found in her poetry. But in her poetry, Dickinson works against them. Predestination seems to her a ruse, compelling man "to choose Himself / His Preappointed Pain" (P 910). She denies the justice of the unredeemed evil suffered by the damned, while feeling a certain sympathy with the reprobate:

> Not probable—The barest Chance—
> A smile too few—a word too much
> And far from Heaven as the Rest—
> The Soul so close on Paradise—
>
> What if the Bird from journey far—
> Confused by Sweets—as Mortals—are—
> Forget the secret of His wing
> And perish—but a Bough between—
> Oh, Groping feet—
> Oh Phantom Queen!   [P 346]

That any given soul could be "far from Heaven as the Rest" is indeed the probability within Calvin's doctrine of reprobation. The divine decree asserts that it is impossible to foreknow which soul may be among the elect. Michael Wigglesworth, in his once popular *Day of Doom*, proclaims:

> Earth's dwellers all, both great and small,
>   have wrought iniquity,
> And suffer must, for it is just,
>   Eternal misery.[29]

And according to Wigglesworth, "The godly wife conceives no grief . . . For the sad state of her dear mate" when the latter has been consigned to the flames. Isaac Watts, too, sings, "Broad is the Road that leads to Death, / And thousands walk together there" (189). Dickinson similarly writes, "The Road to Paradise is plain, And holds scarce one." But she adds, in what suggests (as so often happens) a parody of Watts, "Not me—nor you" (P 1491). Dickinson's own doubts of election are dramatized in the well-known (although perhaps apocryphal) anecdote of her Holyoke years, where she is said, on Miss Lyon's request for all who follow Christ to rise, to have alone remained seated. In a letter of the period she calls herself "one of the lingering bad ones" (L 36), and is said to "still appear unconcerned" in the face of the ongoing revivals and meetings of the school.[30]

For Dickinson, too, heaven is "Not probable." But the poem questions more than her own election. It suggests, in the trivial nature of damning offenses, doubt of the scheme itself. "A smile too few—a word too much," and redemption vanishes. The second stanza develops this criticism. The bird, with "but a Bough between" its journey's progress and its end, will perish, for it has been "Confused by Sweets—as Mortals—are." The good things of this world stand as the gravest threat to hope of the world to come. The edict is severe. The world seems created for the special purpose of tempting mortals to their damnation. The poem ends with feet groping toward a vanished promise and the queenship of election reduced to a phantom.

Even if the evil suffered by the reprobate remains unredeemed, suffering and sin may still have a place in the redemptive scheme. It can make man more dependent upon, and more sensible of, divine mercy. Jonathan Edwards had insisted on the consciousness of sin as the ground for grace. In a sermon on "Great Guilt No Obstacle to the Pardon of the Returning Sinner," he had preached that

> The psalmist pleads the greatness of his sins as an argument for mercy. . . . We should see our misery, and be sensible of our need for mercy; They who are not sensible of their misery cannot truly look to God for mercy; for it is the very notion of divine mercy, that it is the goodness and grace of God to the miserable. . . . They must be sensible that they are not worthy that God should have mercy on them.[31]

F. D. Huntington, in a book of sermons Emily received from her father, equally insisted that sin is "a fact pervading the world, . . . the greatest of evils, and the malignant source of all evils that exist." Sin must be viewed not as a trivial offense, but as utter depravity. A profound "individual conviction of sin" is the first and necessary step "in passing into a new and Christian life." And Huntington urges that

> the first word of the new dispensation was "Repent," and its consummation was the cross built on Calvary to assure forgiveness to "repentance toward God and faith toward our Lord Jesus Christ;" . . . for all the ministrations of our religion presuppose that we all have sinned, and are sinners still.[32]

Dickinson duly exercises the introspection enjoined by Edwards and Huntington. But her response toward the salvific force of penitence, like that toward the justice of eternal punishment, is skeptical:

Remorse—is Memory—awake—
Her Parties all astir—
A Presence of Departed Acts—
At window—and at Door—

Its Past—set down before the Soul
And lighted with a Match—
Perusal—to facilitate—
And help Belief to stretch—

Remorse is cureless—the Disease
Not even God—can heal—
For 'tis His institution—and
The Adequate of Hell—   [P 744]

Introspection is meant to produce in the Christian "a more living sense of his evils" and thereby a "penitential frame" in preparation for spiritual renewal.[33] For Dickinson, however, inward meditation leads toward other ends. She feels her past deeds to be present, as she ought, and engages in their minute perusal. The purpose of the exercise is, as it ought to be, to "help Belief to stretch." But this witness of the spirit, opening the soul to the ministrations of that Physician who heals all ills, becomes instead an antiwitness. Remorse, rather than leading to a cure, itself becomes the disease. The divine power to heal and redeem suffering becomes instead the source of illness and of pain. The process of introspection is reversed. Saving penitence becomes indistinguishable from the hell it should defeat.

Calvinist theodicy finally does more than posit damnation as divine justice and penitential humility as spiritual awakening. It grants suffering a central place in the pattern of Christian living, as a conforming to Christ's passion. Calvin begins his *Institutes* with the injunction that "each of us must, then, be so stung by the consciousness of his own unhappiness as to attain at least some knowledge of God." He later urges Christians to embrace their suffering, for "the more we are afflicted with adversities, the more surely our fellowship with Christ is confirmed."[34] The life of Christ is the model for the life of every Christian, and, as his "was nothing but a sort of perpetual cross" culminating in Calvary, so the Christian should devote himself to the exercise of inward self-denial and outward cross-bearing:

It is principally in His bearing the cross and patient submission to His suffering that Christ is the mirror of sanctity and the example man is to imitate, for God has predestined all whom He adopts as his children to be conformed to the image of Jesus Christ, especially in this matter of bearing their cross as Christ bore his.[35]

Afflictions are to be embraced as integral to the process of sanctification. They promote the obedience and submission conducive to the state of grace. Without cross bearing, there can be no redemption in Christ. And the joy of redemption is "always enough to compensate for the bitterness of the cross."[36]

Dickinson was herself particularly familiar with "The old—road—through pain." And this road, she at times sincerely asserts, is one "That stops—at—Heaven" (P 344). She had read in Huntington's sermons: "Ye shall have tribulation; for it is through much tribulation that any soul entereth into the kingdom of heaven . . . [for Christ] means to show us the ultimate joy to be gained by the suffering." He continues:

Take up [the Cross] in Christ's name, bear it for his sake, and it is light. . . . So Paul bore the Cross of Christ and said of it, "God forbid that I should glory anything but that, boast of anything but that infamy, count anything gain but that loss, be proud of anything but that humiliation.[37]

The lesson is urged in a Watts hymn as well, in diction startlingly Dickinsonian:

When I survey the wondrous Cross
On which the Prince of glory died
My richest gain I count but loss
And pour contempt on all my pride.

Forbid it, Lord that I should boast,
Save in the death of Christ, my Lord;
All the vain things that charm me most
I sacrifice them to His blood.   [515]

Dickinson had little sympathy with the doctrines of reprobation and of utter depravity. But the assurance that suffering is integral to and glorified by a final joy, as of salvation, profoundly engaged her.

"The hallowing of Pain," she writes, "Like hallowing of Heaven, / Obtains at a corporeal Cost" (P 772). She has before her the example of Christ, who "gave away his Life / To Us" (P 567). She has the example of those martyrs who follow Christ "Through the strait pass of suffering" (P 792). And she asserts that pain, if borne with the "strait renunciation" of the "Son of God," becomes a "Sacrament" (P 527). Divine mercy then counters and subsumes the evils endured on earth, making them a gift rather than a burden. Then, it is indeed a "Joy to have merited the Pain / To merit the Release" (P 788). This theodicy underlies, for Dickinson, the entire possiblity of endowing suffering with significance, and to it she devotes considerable attention. She does so, first, on a personal level and sometimes with success.

More often, however, sustained treatments of the theodicean structure reveal an emerging sense of its contradictions. Richard Sewall discusses in detail Dickinson's fascination with Thomas a Kempis, whose *Imitation of Christ* she received as a Christmas gift from Susan Gilbert Dickinson in 1876, although there is evidence she had read the text with care in its 1857 edition. Her copy of the *Imitation*, now in the Yale University library, shows that the chapter on the Cross is the most heavily marked. There she read: "See how in the Cross all things consist, and in dying on it all things depend. There is no other way to life and to true inner peace, than the way of the Cross and of daily self-denial. . . . And if you share his sufferings, you will also share his glory." Sewall accepts this, if not as a doctrine, at least as a structure "very close to Emily's lifelong experience of the Cross and her sense of its meaning."[38] But the *Imitation* cannot be cited as a model for Dickinson without a consciousness of her ironies, not only with regard to the doctrine of the Cross, but also with regard to the assumptions implicit in it. The theodicy the *Imitation* offers deeply moved her. But her verse repeatedly projects a dissatisfaction with the elements constituting its pattern:

Fitter to see Him, I may be
For the long Hindrance—Grace—to Me—
With Summers, and with Winters, grow,
Some passing Year—A trait bestow

To make Me fairest of the Earth—
The Waiting—then—will seem so worth
I shall impute with half a pain
The blame that I was chosen—then—

Time to anticipate His Gaze—
It's first—Delight—and then—Surprise—
The turning o'er and o'er my face
For Evidence it be the Grace—

He left behind One Day—So less
He seek Conviction, That—be This—

The benefit of hindrance and of painful delay is first argued. The
long waiting has made the poet fitter. It has rendered her "fairest"
and not only worthy of grace but more sensible of its worth. This
declared value of pain is, however, complicated from the outset: first
by a subtle insistence that pain is not entirely forgotten in the joy of
reward, and then, by an oblique suggestion that the Redeemer's scrutiny may be overly rigorous. In these opening stanzas, the "Waiting,"
although worthwhile, only assuages "half" the pain of delay. Some
"blame" at being chosen after prolonged suspense remains. And if it
be true that one day less would have weakened the divine "Conviction" of the poet's merit, the incessant search for "Evidence" of election seems scrupulous to the point of pettiness. This possibility grows
pronounced in the poem's conclusion:

I only must not grow so new
That He'll mistake—and ask for me
Of me—when first unto the Door
I go—to Elsewhere go no more—

I only must not change so fair
He'll sigh—"The Other—She—is Where?"
The Love, tho', will array me right
I shall be perfect—in His sight—

If He perceive the other Truth—
Upon an Excellenter Youth—

How sweet I shall not lack in Vain—
But gain—thro' loss—Through Grief—obtain—
The Beauty that reward Him best—
The Beauty of Demand—at Rest—   [P 968]

Anxiety now makes itself felt. Perhaps in his scrutiny, God will discover some flaw to bar the poet from entering heaven. Perhaps, in the time of delay, she will alter and become less rather than more worthy. The poem vacillates between assurance that love "will array me right" and doubt lest perfection and truth be finally perceived in "Excellenter Youth." Love may finally be outweighed by a justice without mercy. And if, at the end, the poet's lack, grief, and loss are declared means to attainment and gain, the redemption thus obtained remains a strange one: "The Beauty of Demand—at Rest." The greatest reward in redemption is that the scrutiny, severity, and demands of the Redeemer will at last cease.

Such hesitation entering into what may at first appear a positive assertion of gain in loss is characteristic of Dickinson. Dickinson will write: "I rose—because He sank" (P 616). But she does not overlook the fact that gain, although it may finally displace loss, is first its ground. As such, gain creates the possibility of loss, and the eventual gain may itself remain inaccessible, only making the actual loss more acute. Thus, sunlight makes the poet's "shade," otherwise bearable, into a "newer Wilderness" (P 1233). Without the experience—or the suspicion—of possession, deprivation is impossible, even as a category. And what possession ultimately bestows may be no more than a painful knowledge:

None can experience stint
Who Bounty—have not known—
The fact of Famine—could not be
Except for Fact of Corn—

Want—is a meagre Art
Acquired by Reverse—
The Poverty that was not Wealth—
Cannot be Indigence.   [P 771]

Recompense is posited here: an art is "Acquired by Reverse." But it is the art of want, of stint, of famine. Attainment then becomes but

82

another element in the economy of indigence. Wealth is subsumed by an implacable poverty. Loss, in an ambiguous and ambivalent role, begins to unravel its ties to the gain that may justify it.

This ambiguity penetrates Dickinson's treatments of personal suffering. It equally penetrates the question of national suffering. When Higginson left to join his regiment, Dickinson wrote to him, "Best gains—must have the Losses' test—to constitute them gains" (L 280). As is often the case, Dickinson seems to assert with regard to war that there is indeed some gain in loss. Yet, especially with regard to war, such assertions prove deceptive. A theodicy of war's suffering which would affirm its contribution to or compensation by some final good seems to Dickinson deeply problematic, as does theodicy of suffering in general. The war in this becomes one of the fields on which Dickinson struggles with her theological conflicts. Theodicean structures constitute that field.

The justification of loss by gain is the essential theodicean structure. And if a positive interpretation can be given to a negative fact, a theodicy is accomplished. In Dickinson's work, although such structures are consistently invoked, they are rarely accomplished or fulfilled. Instead, a disjunction between loss and gain, an inversion of the terms, or a defeat of gain by loss occurs. What appears to be an assertion of value that redeems a negative experience in fact does not do so. Some other term is substituted in place of the expected justification. Dickinson proposes a variety of permutations of the theodicean structure, in which she displaces the concluding redemptive term with one that instead defeats redemption. The structure of redemption itself is consequently undermined.

Of the fact of pain as such, Dickinson had much consciousness and little doubt. Her meditations on it are many and precise:

Pain—expands the Time—
Ages coil within
The minute Circumference
Of a single Brain—

Pain contracts—the Time—
Occupied with Shot
Gamuts of Eternities
Are as they were not—   [P 967]

The sensation of pain emerges as absolute. By its calendar time itself is measured. The eternity that should redeem is instead engulfed by it. Its moment encompasses entire ages. It thus stands only in relation to itself and loses any tie to a possible redemptive term. This account stands as an abstract, almost mathematical formula. But while little specific content is given to the "Ages" defined by pain, there is a suggestion of history. The "Time" of pain, so all-containing, is "Occupied with Shot." Gunfire fills its moment.

The suggestion of gunfire here becomes in other poems a more specific imagery. And the stark pronouncement of pain gives way to attempts to place it within some redemptive structure, albeit with uncertain success:

> Success is counted sweetest
> By those who ne'er succeed.
> To comprehend a nectar
> Requires sorest need.

> Not one of all the purple Host
> Who took the Flag today
> Can tell the definition
> So clear of Victory

> As he defeated—dying—
> On whose forbidden ear
> The distant strains of triumph
> Break agonized and clear.   [P 67]

"To comprehend a nectar / Requires sorest need." Dickinson seems to be asserting that even need has value. Experience of the worst, she suggests, heightens the experience of the good. "Water is taught by thirst. . . . Peace—by its battles told" (P 135), she writes elsewhere. Through thirst, we comprehend a nectar; through failure, success; through defeat, victory. Without this perspective, victory and success would not exist as terms. In this poem, nevertheless, the agony of defeat, the loss of life, speak stronger than does the comprehension gained thereby. The sense of exclusion, of want, of heartbreaking disappointment is not canceled by the clarity of vision achieved through it. That clear vision instead emerges as one of defeat, of need, of death. These have led to an increased appreciation of success or of victory, but only in terms of the fuller cognizance of their inaccessibility. The clear "definition" of victory is a definition of its lack.

Therefore, the poem poses rather than answers the question of value. In doing so, it lays a snare difficult to evade and often succumbed to. Richard Wilbur, after considering how the poem impresses us "with the wretchedness of the dying soldier's lot" and conceding that "an improved understanding of the nature of victory may seem small compensation," goes on to assert that the "increase of awareness" that attends defeat and death is, to Dickinson, "the better bargain." The poem is proposed as an instance of Dickinson's "sumptuous despair" in which privation "is more plentiful than plenty." Wilbur thus accepts Dickinson's apparent arguments that "every evil" confers "some balancing good."[39]

But in "Success," the argument of compensation serves to dramatize the agony of deprivation, made more tangible when seen against a posited justification. "Success" finally concludes with a finer, more poignant description of defeat, as Margaret Homans explains. Homans, in *Women Writers and Poetic Identity*, examines the rhetorical pattern in which Dickinson counterposes opposites toward a seeming reconciliation. This often results, however, in a disguised irony, as occurs in "Success": "the poem is surely a bitter parody . . . of orthodox thinking," in which Dickinson, instead of finding "a balance of price and purchase . . . finds an equivalence of valuelessness."[40] The poem's vision of victory is not really a newly defined value which can be attributed to the experience of the defeated. The greater knowledge gotten through the "distant strains of triumph" hardly comforts the ear for which it is forbidden. It is perhaps clearer to the dying than to the victors, but it is no less agonized thereby.

In place of a theodicean term by which defeat is justified, the poem concludes with defeat itself: a term that is redundant rather than redemptive. "Success" adopts martial imagery for this undermined theodicean structure. But Dickinson applies this redundant structure to nonmartial situations as well:

Despair's advantage is achieved
By suffering—Despair—
To be assisted of Reverse
One must Reverse have bore—

The Worthiness of Suffering like
The Worthiness of Death
Is ascertained by tasting—

As can no other Mouth

Of Savors—make us conscious—
As did ourselves partake—
Affliction feels impalpable
Until Ourselves are struck—   [P 799]

We cannot fully understand despair or suffering, the poet asserts, unless we ourselves have experienced it. The poem further promises that this experience will benefit us. There is an "advantage" to despair. Reverse can assist. The "Worthiness" of suffering and of death imply that these have worth. This implicit promise is strengthened by the image of tasting. We know a flavor only when we ourselves have sampled it: clearly a desirable attainment that justifies the venture. But this image proves misleading. No such positive worth is finally attributed to despair or to death. In the end, the poem leaves us with the stark facts of them. "Affliction feels impalpable / Until Ourselves are struck," the poem concludes. Suffering is not fully impressed upon us until we ourselves confront it. But once it has been confronted, it does not become some inestimable lesson. It remains the experience of suffering in all its unqualified simplicity. "Pain comes from the darkness," writes Randall Jarrell, "and we call it wisdom. It is pain." Dickinson refuses to name suffering by any euphemism. In this poem, where "Advantage" should be, there is only despair, the very term with which the poem began. There is no redemption, only redundance.

Theodicy, when so treated, is given an ironic form. The term that resolves misfortune does so without redeeming it. In Dickinson, the ironies are multiple. Sometimes, she replaces the theodicean term that would justify a negative fact with the negative fact itself, resulting in a redundant structure. At other times, she further intensifies the redundance:

We learn in the Retreating
How vast an one

Was recently among us—
A Perished Sun

Endear in the departure
How doubly more
Than all the Golden presence
It was—before—   [P 1083]

Retreat, rather than defeat, is Dickinson's martial, negative trope
here. And the poem ostensibly argues, at least at the outset, that
retreat has heuristic value. From its loss we "learn" the value of one
"recently among us." But the second stanza twists the assertion. If a
greater sense of worth has been attained, it has been attained at
double cost. We no longer have the "Golden presence," and we miss as
well the value we have come to attribute to it in its loss. Gain makes
loss greater. It is not a restoration, but an intensification of lack. "Lost
doubly—but by contrast—most," the poet writes (P 953). The "doubly more" is the value first lost and then, because valued through loss,
felt as loss even more.

Redundance here is multiplied. Absence not only defeats presence,
but negates it twofold. And redundance can then give way to a resolving term which rather than reiterating the initial loss, substitutes for
it a term still worse. The ironic theodicean structure then proceeds by
displacing the term that should redeem by one of greater negativity:

If any sink, assure that this, now standing—
Failed like Themselves—and conscious that it rose—
Grew by the Fact, and not the Understanding
How Weakness passed—or Force—arose—

Tell that the Worst, is easy in a Moment—
Dread, but the Whizzing, before the Ball—
When the Ball enters, enters Silence—
Dying—annuls the power to kill.   [P 358]

Dickinson here returns to a literal battlefield as her theodicean
problem. The first stanza defines this problem in a series of images
where a negative term is balanced against a positive one meant to
vindicate it. Descent is linked to ascent, failure to resurgence. Those

who "sink" can again be "standing," those who have risen had once "Failed." Deplorable situations have been righted, either through the passing of "Weakness" or the advent of "Force."

The second stanza promises to continue this movement. The worst is posited with the assurance that it will be "easy in a Moment." Dickinson now presents her foremost image of the worst. It is "Dread" as the "Whizzing, before the Ball." Consistency with the first stanza demands that this dread gunfire should be vindicated by some positive term. The term, however, proves to be simply death. This represents another permutation in a theodicean structure. The negative term has given way, not to a positive one, but to a term more negative still. The bullet's entry relieves the dread of its approach. The resolution to fear is death: a kind of release, it is true, but hardly one that transforms dread into a positive experience. The worst has given way, then, not to something better, but to something even more terrible. The poem's conclusion reinforces the irony. The positive value of death is that "Dying—annuls the power to kill." Comfort is the negation of a negative condition, not the assertion of a positive one. The only justification for death in war is that it precludes more murder. This ironic theodicy is the very best that can be said of war.

Commentators on Dickinson often assume that she wrote during a period of religious decline and that her religious doubts are its reflection in her mind's capsule. According to Henry Wells,

> Emily Dickinson embodied in a heightened form the fatality of her age, wherein religion became less a normal function of the human soul than an agonized problem in human morbidity. Throughout the civilized world . . . the foundations of faith were shaken.[41]

Dickinson's has been repeatedly called a "literary Protestantism,"[42] and Calvinism, for Edward Taylor, Solomon Stoddard, and Jonathan Edwards, as well as for Dickinson, a theology "essentially esthetic."[43] Religious decline was, however, far from straightforward or steady. Certainly, an encroaching process of secularization is visible in nineteenth-century America, reflected not least in the revisions given to traditional Calvinsim by the Unitarians and the Transcendentalists. Nevertheless, Dickinson's Amherst had remained rooted in the older Puritan tradition, even aggressively so. The avowed purpose of the churches in western Massachusetts was to uphold what was thought to be true religion against liberalizing movements.[44] And it was not only in Amherst that religious revivals swept many to conversion.

The decline of Calvinism is not the dominant note apparent in Dickinson's period, whatever deeper forces were working to undermine orthodoxy. Indeed, especially in the years preceding the Civil War, the atmosphere in the country was one of religious zeal and nationalism. And even those movements that represented incursions into older Calvinist creeds did so by way of transformation rather than exorcism. Perry Miller, Ernest Tuveson, Sacvan Bercovitch and others persuasively argue the persistence of the older Puritan modes of thought and discourse into the nineteenth century. "The fathers had provided the pattern and established the direction," writes Bercovitch, and "by all historical accounts, the enthusiasm contributed directly to the Civil War."[45] If the nineteenth century also witnessed new theological movements espousing the benevolence of God, the natural ability of man to do good, and the merely apparent existence of evil,[46] both the rhetorical structures and the concerns of Calvinism persisted into the war era. Even transcendentalists responded to the Civil War, according to Robert Albrecht, by reverting "to the religious concepts they had apparently rejected years before, . . . preaching that the war was a remission by blood for the salvation of man and nation."[47]

Nor was the older conception of evil eradicated by a new emphasis on man's perfectibility. What F. O. Mathiesson calls Hawthorne's and Melville's "reaffirmation of tragedy" approached the Calvinist doctrine of fallen nature with seriousness.[48] Melville himself cites the "great power of blackness" as his original attraction to Hawthorne— a power that "derives its force from its appeal to that Calvinist sense of Innate Depravity and Original Sin from whose visitations in some shape or other no deeply thinking mind is always and wholly free."[49] And Hawthorne, in *The Marble Faun*, poses the problem of evil with the preciseness of a metaphysician:

> Is sin, then—which we deem such a dreadful blackness in the universe—is it, like sorrow, merely an element of human education, through which we struggle to a higher and purer state then we could

89

otherwise have attained? Did Adam fall, that we might ultimately rise to a far loftier paradise than his?[50]

On these grounds the quarrel with Emerson erupted. Emerson, of all the Transcendentalists, did attempt formulations more consistent with his enlightened religion than with orthodoxy, even in the crisis of war. He would speak in terms of moral triumph rather than religious redemption. To him the war was a "battle for Humanity" rather than one for salvation.[51] Still, the conceptual structures remain religious in addressing evil and invoking redemptions—a religion that, however, seemed to Melville deficient in malignity. Melville's annotations to the *Essays* take urgent issue with Emerson's dictum—"The first lesson of history is the good of evil"—protesting that Emerson "must make that good somehow against the eternal hell itself."[52]

At issue is Emerson's own doctrine of compensation, which has often been compared to Dickinson's. "All things are moral," Emerson writes. "A perfect equity adjusts its balance in all parts of life." What seems an "unpaid loss" is part of the "deep remedial force that underlies all facts." For "evil is good in the making. . . . If limitation is power that shall be, calamities, oppositions and weights are wings and means, we are reconciled."[53] Such reconciliations to loss as seem expressed here have been attributed to Dickinson as well—even at Emerson's expense. Karl Keller, who calls Emerson's compensation a "sentimental eschatology" sees Dickinson as insisting on "the cultivation of deprivation to heighten the hope," and even as finding "hope and faith possible only in hell." For "hell has its esthetic purposes."[54] According to Keller, suffering for Emerson becomes a blithe excuse for unfounded optimism; for Dickinson, it is a welcome aid to aesthetic production which subsumes all moral questions.

These assertions tend to oversimplify both Emerson's and Dickinson's theodicies. Emerson's consciousness of evil is perhaps greater than has been assumed. His essay on "The Tragic" opens with the assertion that half the universe is a "House of Pain," that "in the dark hours our existence seems to be a defensive war, a great struggle against the encroaching All, which threatens surely to engulf us soon, and is impatient of our short reprieve." And if, in the course of the essay, he hastens to add that "time consoles," that the intellect forms a "region whereunto these passionate clouds of sorrow cannot rise," the assertion seems somewhat a rearguard action.[55] In "Experience," Emerson can "grieve that grief can teach me nothing," but irony immediately follows: "Nothing is left us now but death. We look to that with a grim satisfaction, saying, there at least is reality that will not dodge us."[56]

It is not only that we prefer Emerson at his most apocalyptic, as Harold Bloom suggests, but that his insistence on moral law seems something of a desperate act.[57] Dickinson's treatments of evil were no less so. She, like Emerson, profoundly wished to find compensating good in evil.[58] She constantly searched for it and asserted its pattern, but she rarely found it. Nor did she see the world's suffering as justified by contributing to her poetic powers. A profound awareness of pain often inspired her to write. But her writing represented a bitter struggle with suffering and evil, not their justification. Only a faith in moral law, such as Emerson defined, would suffice.

The possibility of such a faith stands at the center of Dickinson's religious conflicts—conflicts that the Civil War could only have augmented. The bloodshed of the war itself would challenge both orthodoxy's assertions of providential suffering and the assertions of benevolent nature and perfectable man espoused by orthodoxy's critics. That bloodshed was cataclysmic. Of a population of 30 million, 500,000 men were killed. Some regiments lost 75 or 80 percent of their enlisted men. Some battles claimed 25 percent of their combatants. The Civil War marked an increase in military violence that presaged the violence of war in our own century. Bruce Catton further argues that the Civil War introduced a new era of dehumanized warfare. New technology led to the replacement of personal encounter by anonymous battles. Moreover, like the wars that succeeded it, the Civil War was a war of "unpredictable results and unlimited objectives." According to Catton, it transformed the society which had entered into it in ways unforeseen and was limited in its violence not by any sense of moral restraint but only by the "technical capacity to do harm."[59]

This violence was proclaimed by religious nationalists as a Holy Crusade. The rhetoric of religion had been used to justify an outbreak of what Edmund Wilson calls patriotic gore. It even helped to pro-

mote this outbreak. This would not have strengthened Dickinson's
already hesitating faith. Nor would it have encouraged her to employ
traditional religious formulas to justify a war in which religion itself
played so crucial a role. The contradiction of holy destruction can be
felt throughout Dickinson's appraisal, not only of the war, but of the
religious principles underlying its interpretations. As such, the conflict radiates outward and can be felt in her work, at times, in unexpected ways:

> My Life had stood—a Loaded Gun—
> In Corners—till a Day
> The Owner passed—identified—
> And carried Me away—
>
> And now We roam in Sovereign Woods—
> And now We hunt the Doe—
> And every time I speak for Him—
> The Mountains straight reply—
>
> And do I smile, such cordial light
> Upon the Valley glow—
> It is as a Vesuvian face
> Had let its pleasure through—
>
> And when at Night—Our good Day done—
> I guard My Master's Head—
> 'Tis better than the Eider-Duck's
> Deep Pillow—to have shared—
>
> To foe of His—I'm deadly foe—
> None stir the second time—
> On whom I lay a Yellow Eye—
> Or an emphatic Thumb—
>
> Though I than He—may longer live
> He longer must—than I—
> For I have but the power to kill,
> Without—the power to die—   [P 754]

This poem has prompted many interpretations, which invariably
posit Dickinson's psychic life—with regard to poetic, sexual, and/or
aggressive energy—as the poem's subject. Its allegory is read accord-

ingly. To Charles Anderson, the Owner is a beloved; the Loaded Gun, "the charged potential of the human being who remains dormant until identified into conscious vitality."[60] To Thomas Johnson, the poet is assessing her poetic achievement, with the poet and her creative power the respective allegorical terms.[61] David Porter similarly sees the gun as "the instrument of language" and the poem as "an allegory, almost pure in self-regard, of language speaking itself."[62] John Cody accepts both the sexual and the poetic readings, but subsumes them into a psychoanalytic reading that emphasizes the link between the "wish to love, to be sexual, to be creative," and "a furious propensity to destroy." The Owner is then "the directing, executive, volitional function," the Gun, "the aggressive, destructive, and erotic impulses."[63] And according to Sharon Cameron, aggressive instinct finally becomes the death instinct and the poem "concerned with the way in which death confers both knowledge and power."[64]

The poem, however, while involving these various psychic forces, may be more literal than has been assumed. Written in 1863, it is perhaps not merely gratuitous that the poem posits firearms as its controlling figure. In this light, the poem's religious resonances may also be taken literally. Preachers were repeatedly insisting that war is a manifestation of divine power, and man, God's instrument in waging it. This could suggest, in a reading posed and rightly dismissed by Cameron, that "picked up by God, the speaker becomes His marksman."[65] For the poem's final recalcitrant stanza—the proof text of any reading—will not sustain the assertion that mortal man has "but the power to kill without the power to die." This seems, instead, a description of the Deity himself—who, like the Gun, has power over life and death and, like the Gun, is himself immortal.

A radical inversion is here implied. The poem's speaker would not be the poet or any human agent, but God; and the poem would examine divine power in conjunction with human agency. Such power is variously suggested. In the second stanza, woods and mountains resound with the Gun's power—a psalmic trope found, for example, in Isaac Watts:

> From mountains near the sky
> Let His high praise resound
> From humble shrubs and cedars high
> And vales and fields around. [54]

That power should also conjoin with wrath is typical of the hymnal and the Bible. For Watts, mountains "shake like frightened sheep" (471). Or as Isaiah prophesies:

> Therefore I will shake the heavens, and the earth shall remove out of her place, in the wrath of the Lord of hosts, and in the day of his fierce anger. And it shall be as the chased doe, and as a sheep that no man taketh up: They shall every man turn to his own people, and flee every one into his own land. [13:13–14]

Dickinson's mountains, like Isaiah's earth, echo with a power that hunts the doe. In the poem, ominous wrath comes in this way to undermine glory. The valley glows at the smile of the All-powerful, but the face remains Vesuvian. The "good Day done" of clerical rhetoric evinces the security felt by those who bestow themselves to heavenly keeping upon lying down to sleep. But here the guardian is lethal.

This power, at least as dreadful as it is majestic, becomes, with the poem's inversion, a human implement. Here, man is not God's instrument, but God man's. In Watts's hymn "For a day of Prayer in time of War," God is called upon to "inspire our armies for the fight" so that "our foes shall fall and die with shame" (602). And the Lord responds: "My sword shall boast its thousands slain / And drink the blood of haughty kings." Here, too, the Gun "to foe of His" is "deadly foe." The Yellow Eye would indeed be deadly if it, as in Watts, "with infinite survey does the world behold" (14) and the thumb, emphatic if found on an Omnipotent hand. But the foe, now, is chosen not by a divine but by a human master—a danger perhaps inherent in the topos of a militant church. Murder committed in God's name—as was certainly the case with both northern and southern crusaders—may imply a terrible misuse of heavenly power.

This the poem's conclusion, as parodic rhetoric, suggests:

> Though I than He may longer live
> He longer must—than I
> For I have but the power to kill
> Without the power to die.

Divinity surely lives longer than do mortals. Here, it may be that the divine Gun can deprive of life while remaining immune to death's power. On these grounds, it is further suggested that "He"—here, mortal man—must live longer than the immortal weapon he wields. Perhaps an ascendancy of the human over the divine is intended. Perhaps man, although killing, also experiences death, granting him a certain equity denied to the Gun. Dickinson had earlier written: "Dying—annuls the power to kill" (P 358). This annulment never overtakes the destructive Creator. That man dies emerges here, as in the earlier poem, as the only positive term—which remains, however, negative. But even that inversion is overshadowed by the poem's central tension and contradiction—that the everliving kills, that the Creator is destructive. The strange counterpoint between innocence and murder for which this poem is famous becomes functional and systematic in the framework of a martial God—who, during the time of this poem's composition, was a concrete and historical, not just a figurative, Being.

The poem's own final attack is directed against that Power which destroys. It may be that man appropriates power to do evil in God's name. But God here seems most blameworthy in the very nature of his power, which is not merely open to misuse, but has wrathful and destructive elements inherent in it. These elements were certainly made painfully evident by the war. And whether the poem is read finally in terms of psychic or divine forces, the problem of destructive power in the order of the world and, therefore, of the contradictions involved in a benevolent and omnipotent God remains preeminent for Dickinson. It extends beyond the fact of war, which finally becomes an instance—and at times a model—for Dickinson's confrontation with evil and suffering. And the theodicy invoked for war, as for suffering in general, becomes less and less satisfactory. War emerges as one aspect of a problem that has for Dickinson broader implications. The ironies that emerge consistently when war is addressed equally emerge when theodicy is treated as a general structure:

> I should have been too glad, I see—
> Too lifted—for the scant degree
> Of Life's penurious Round—
> My little Circuit would have shamed
> This new Circumference—have blamed—
> The homelier time behind.

I should have been too saved—I see—
Too rescued—Fear too dim to me
That I could spell the Prayer
I knew so perfect—yesterday—
That Scalding One—Sabachthani—
Recited fluent—here—

Earth would have been too much—I see—
And Heaven—not enough for me—
I should have had the Joy
Without the Fear—to justify—
The Palm—without the Calvary—
So Savior—Crucify—

Defeat—whets Victory—they say—
The Reefs—in old Gethsemane—
Endear the Coast—beyond!
'Tis Beggars—Banquets—can define—
'Tis Parching—vitalizes Wine—
"Faith" faints—to understand.   [P 313]

This poem contrasts two different frameworks or points of view: the viewpoint the poet in fact possesses and the one she projects and asserts ought to have been hers. The poet "should have been too glad" to have been burdened by what now appears as "Life's penurious Round." She "should have been too saved" to have felt the fears she in fact does feel. "I should have had the Joy / Without the Fear—to justify." As in other theodicean poems, the poet contrasts the negative terms of penury and fear with the positive terms of gladness, salvation, and joy. And she refuses to integrate the negative terms into the positive ones. The joy she names does not succeed in justifying her fear. She remains with the terror it should have assuaged and with a penury it does not explain.

The structure in which she finds herself thus neither assuages nor justifies. And she specifies this structure. From her projected framework, there should be no need to "spell the Prayer . . . Sabachthani," Christ's cry to God of being forsaken. From her projected framework, she should have "The Palm—without the Calvary." Dickinson here is questioning the Passion of Christ as an emblem of Salvation. The image of redemption on the cross should assure not only that "the drama [of history] have a happy ending, but the happy ending had been implicit in the beginning and made possible by it."[66] But Dickinson is questioning Christ's suffering and triumph, Calvary and palm, as a pattern of theodicy.

Instead, she asserts what she feels ought to be her framework in place of the theodicean framework which seems wanting: "Earth would have been too much—I see— / And Heaven—not enough for me." Dickinson is proposing a structure in which earth would in itself suffice and heaven would be insufficient. There would then be no need for a mediation between a fallen world and a redeeming heaven. The conditions of earth would be explained according to some immanent structure. This structure the poet does not delineate here. She only calls it a "new Circumference," which would put the present "little Circuit" to shame. She does, however, define her critique of traditional Christian theodicy in the final stanza, which reiterates the Dickinsonian pattern of loss and gain:

Defeat—whets Victory—they say—
The Reefs—in old Gethsemane—
Endear the Coast—beyond!
'Tis Beggars—Banquets—can define—
'Tis Parching—vitalizes Wine—
"Faith" faints—to understand.

Lack is vindicated because it contributes to and is finally subsumed into a redeeming result. At least, this is what "they say." But the distance between the evil and the good is exceedingly difficult to negotiate. The different terms do not cohere. The vision of heaven does not sufficiently explain the terrestrial world. The relation between the coast beyond and the present reefs is far from clear. The justification seems inadequate, and the evil, arbitrary. " 'Faith' " cannot meet these demands.

The critique of theodicy finally implicates, for Dickinson, the whole structure of relation between redemption and travail, heaven and earth. Much of Dickinson's poetry expresses her efforts to define the new circumference she names here as a system in which contradictory and painful experiences could be placed and explained. And much of her work explores her doubts concerning transcendent promises, as they actually function within the immanent world. The poem, too, suggests some of the sources for Dickinson's doubts. This is not a poem about war. "Defeat—whets Victory" is only one among several images of loss and gain and is drawn from traditional religious rhetoric. But in a poem written in 1862, when religious, martial rhetoric had literal military application, the resonance is ominous. Dickinson's religious doubts became acute, or at least expressed, at a time of violence in which religion was implicated. The Civil War, as a war of religious rhetoric, helped undermine that rhetoric as a justification of evil. As a way of God, it helped cast doubt on his ways.

Four

Metaphysical Revolt

The playwright who wrote the folio of this world and wrote it badly
(He gave us light first and the sun two days later) the Lord of things as
they are whom the most Roman of Catholics call *dio boia*, hangman
god, is doubtless all in all in all of us.

—James Joyce, *Ulysses*

The headings under which Dickinson's verse is typically categorized—"love," "life," "nature," "immortality"[1]—omit her pervasive and possibly central poetic mode, that of blasphemy. Dickinson's
meditations upon nature, life, immortality, and even love are informed, and often structured by, attempts to align the sphere of
human experience with that of divine activity. These spheres seemed
to her hardly to concur. Against divine benevolence stood earthly
suffering; against divine power, man's inability to comprehend its
exercise; against a supposed order encompassing heaven and earth,
an empirical perception of a state that seemed to Dickinson to border
on chaos. These contradictions led her to confront, and ultimately to
attack, the structures that posited them, becoming a source of the
acute tension underlying much of her work.

Within that tension, religious patterns and expectations are posed
against radical doubts as to their coherence and fulfillment. The
religious configurations are not, however, simply repudiated. They
are retained, but are no longer necessarily used as vehicles by which
faith is expressed. Instead, they serve to confute the principles of
belief and are turned toward ends contrary to their normative purpose. The result is an acerbity which is doubly enforced by that
reversal. Seemingly innocent entreaties become assaults. Seemingly
pious forms are appropriated to explode their own premises:

The Heart asks Pleasure—first—
And then—Excuse from Pain—
And then—those little Anodynes
That deaden suffering—

And then—to go to sleep—
And then—if it should be
The will of its Inquisitor
The privilege to die—   [P 536]

This poem opens with a plea, but becomes, through unrelenting progression, a direct assault. The otherworld is sought, as orthodoxy urges. But here, it is sought only as a release from torment. To face death serenely as a just recompense for toil would be seemly. To demand it as a negative state made desirable only in contrast to earthly life transmutes it from something heavenly to something demonic. More demonic still is the God who institutes life as an unendurable agony: for he is the Inquisitor who at the poem's end is revealed as the perpetrator of the poet's condition from the outset. Still, this poem is not a meditation on pain. It is a counterthrust at the notion that in spite of its trials, life is essentially a gift; that suffering should be patiently borne and will be far outweighed by the benefits of the otherworld; and that the otherworld is a joyfully embraced existence.

Such inversion approaches parody. But as with parody, the religious configurations that constitute the poem's model are not entirely dismissed. Religious forms are treated seriously, if only to be defeated. And the poem, in its form, remains an appeal to the divinity it concomitantly scorns. Religion here is not renounced; it is bitterly confronted. The strength of a religious tie is thus conversely asserted. This, when considered with the many poems that assert positive acceptance of immortality—the pivotal point of Dickinson's religious concerns—argues for her genuine need of faith, a need she frequently expresses and defines:

We do not know the time we lose—
The awful moment is
And takes its fundamental place
Among the certainties—

A firm appearance still inflates
The card—the chance—the friend—
The spectre of solidities
Whose substances are sand—   [P 1106]

However uncertain the time of death or what follows it may be, having to confront it "takes its fundamental place / Among the certainties." In light of this definitive and inevitable fact, all temporal things must seem relative and uncertain. The life of a friend is as exposed and as fragile as is mere chance. All that appears solid and substantive ultimately becomes specter and sand.

This sense of mortal instability prompts the poet to insist that those "insecure" like herself—with whatever self-irony this may imply—are those "to whom not any Face cohere / Unless concealed in thee" (P 1499). In the time of a "suffering Summer," she will embrace "the divine words: 'There is a world elsewhere' " (L 557). Without assurance of a divine presence and a divine promise, however imperceptible or uncertain, the present world would be incoherent.

In the face of mortality and sorrow, then, religion seems necessary. But this very necessity forms the ground of its doubt. God, whose benignity and power is the basis of belief in an afterworld, nevertheless veils heaven in mystery after having made man mortal: acts that impugn his good will. Redemption, if it is true, may be a sign of kindness, but the fact that the world is such as to require it casts such kindness into question and weakens it as a premise of belief. Thus the argument returns upon itself:

A Shade upon the mind there passes
As when on Noon
A Cloud the mighty Sun encloses
Remembering

That some there be too numb to notice
Oh God
Why give if Thou must take away
The Loved?   [P 882]

The poet's appeal here is not so much aggressive as impassioned. The natural world provides, as it so often does in Dickinson, an image of man's transitory condition. As the light of noon is clouded, so life is darkened by remembering the dead. And the "Mighty" source of light does nothing to prevent this, for all its power. Indeed, that source, whether the Sun or God, is presented here as the origin of loss as well—a loss so great as almost to annul possession. The sincerity of the question posed at the end establishes this poem as a true attempt to address divinity. But the religious posture is undercut by the nature of the poet's question.

Invocation of religious forms so that they defy rather than affirm belief defines the structure of Dickinson's blasphemies and intensifies her protest. At the same time, it maintains that protest within a religious framework. The poems become scenes of religious struggle rather than of religious abdication. Dickinson rebukes God, but she does not turn away from him. Her poetry turns toward him in protest. It is a contention with God against God and thereby occurs at the level which T. S. Eliot, writing of Baudelaire, describes as genuine: "Genuine blasphemy, genuine in spirit and not purely verbal, is the product of partial belief, and is as impossible to the complete atheist as the perfect Christian. It is a way of affirming belief."[2]

Dickinson's blasphemy does not abjure faith. It strains against a faith in terms of which it nevertheless continues to function. As for Eliot's Baudelaire, there is for Dickinson a "gap between human and divine love." The human love she so feelingly affirms and so painfully misses when it is taken from her seems at odds with heavenly mercy. But Dickinson cannot simply resolve the contradiction by omitting divine love. Instead, she protests the gap between the two and, through blasphemy, attempts to assault it.

That Dickinson's verse variously reflects her dissatisfactions with traditional religious formulations has often been remarked. The state of her soul has long been regarded as an embattled one, however arguments diverge as to her final stance toward her religious doubts. What is less recognized is the degree to which her variety of expression constitutes a sustained and consistent critique of metaphysics. Dickinson's has been called an "amazing inconsistency of intellectual position."[3] David Porter speaks of her "taste for individual excitements as against overall design." He asserts later, "Rather than enacting the choice of a human attitude, her poems speak and speak in the absence of a stance."⁴ But the meditations on religion that seem sporadic or momentary in fact proceed according to definite conceptual categories, which together comprise a coherent, comprehensive criticism of the premises underlying traditional religious assumptions. This criticism derives not only from her personal situation but from weaknesses she felt to be inherent in the metaphysical structure itself. And her poetry, for all its vicissitudes, provides an anatomy of the needs that made her turn toward religion and of her dissatisfaction with the responses it offered her.

Dickinson's imagination inhabits what Northrop Frye has called a "middle earth," above which "is the sky with whatever it reveals or conceals."⁵ It is imperative for her that earth and sky together form a complete pattern, but she is overwhelmed by their isolation from each other. "Heaven—is what I cannot reach," she writes in one poem (P 239). Moon and star are very far, but there is One even farther: "He—is more than a firmament—from Me / So I can never go" (P 240). An immeasurable distance separates her from the divine world. And this is due first to an epistemological problem. Heaven remains a mystery to the living which no knowledge can penetrate. The "Dying Eye" darkens "Without disclosing" death's secret (P 547). The dead "hasten away" to a world of "Secret deep" (L 890). The afterlife is the epitome of unanswerable questions:

Of subjects that resist
Redoubtablest is this
Where go we—
Go we anywhere
Creation after this?   [P 1417]

Lack of knowledge constitutes the first barrier between the poet and heaven. But it is a barrier that could be overcome, if not by knowledge, then by faith. Faith Dickinson describes as the "Pierless Bridge" that supports "what We see / Unto the Scene that We do not" (P 915). Yet Dickinson's faith does not so support her. Heaven's existence becomes a problem because doubts of heaven's role have already shaken the faith that could have sufficed to assure her of it. Underlying Dickinson's epistemological doubts are axiological ones which are far more formidable.

103

For even if heaven should exist, Dickinson questions what relevance it may have for her:

Their Height in Heaven comforts not—
Their Glory—nought to me—
'Twas best imperfect—as it was—
I'm finite—I can't see—

The House of Supposition—
The Glimmering Frontier that
Skirts the Acres of Perhaps—
To Me—shows insecure—

The Wealth I had—contented me—
If 'twas a meaner size—
Then I had counted it until
It pleased my narrow Eyes—

Better than larger values—
That show however true—
This timid life of Evidence
Keeps pleading—"I don't know." [P 696]

Dickinson's doubts of heaven extend in this poem beyond an uncertainty about heaven's existence, although this question is introduced. The "Height" of those in heaven does not comfort in part because as a "finite" being, the poet cannot perceive them there. "Acres of Perhaps" must be crossed before the afterworld's "Frontier" can be reached, and across which it remains a "House of Supposition."

The poem, however, is primarily not as concerned with heaven's actuality as with its nature. The wealth possessed in this world, states the third stanza, although a "meaner size" than that promised by heaven, seems to the poet more fitting. She proceeds to measure it and finds that it pleases her "narrow Eyes." She is contented with what she has. " 'Twas best imperfect as it was" in the first stanza implies this as well, as does the concluding stanza. Although heaven's may be "larger values," those of earth are still "Better," and they are so not only because more certain, but intrinsically. The order of heaven may be too incommensurate with the order of earth to provide consolation. Its grandeur may be such that it is unsuitable to earthly standards. The "I don't know" of the poem's conclusion may then refer not so much to the reality of heaven's rewards but to their relevance. Heavenly glory is "nought" to the poet, not because it may not exist, but because in its height it cannot be applied to earthly existence and makes no difference to it.

To assert that heaven is irrelevant is far more radical than to assert that it is uncertain. But Dickinson argues in poem after poem that comfort in the afterworld is unrelated to human affliction. It comes too late, and by taking place in another world, it does not affect our condition in this one. "On ear too far for the delight, / Heaven beguiles the tired," she writes (P 121). In the next world it may be that "People thirst no more," but she asks:

> Shall We remember Parching—then?
> Those Waters sound so grand—
> I think a little Well—like Mine—
> Dearer to understand—   [P 460]

Waters meted out after thirst has gone are mistimed. Such retribution no longer engages the problem it was supposed to assuage. It would be more praiseworthy had water been provided here. Dickinson therefore questions the value of heavenly promises and the whole framework in which they are offered:

> Is Heaven a Physician?
> They say that He can heal—
> But Medicine Posthumous
> Is unavailable—
>
> Is Heaven an Exchequer?
> They speak of what we owe—
> But that negotiation
> I'm not a Party to—   [P 1270]

Posthumous medicine is unavailable to the living, and the dead no longer need it. Divine rewards are not administered when they are required. God's role is relegated to the next world. This seems to the poet a failure of God to fulfill his responsibilities. Therefore, she questions whether she need be responsible to him. The whole basis of human/divine transaction is questionable. Heaven is an "Exchequer" which can call men to account, but Dickinson doubts the terms of the transaction and resists entering into it.

Commercial language is not out of place here; Dickinson often employs it. To her, God is a "thrifty Deity" (P 724), a "Banker" as much as a "Father" (P 49), who presides as an "Auctioneer" at death, selling the "prices of Despair" (P 1612). Her part in the world to come she calls "shares in Primrose Banks" with God supplying the "Bond" of guarantee (P 247). This mercantile diction is consistent with the language of her day and of its conception of divine/human interchange. In the America of her period, economic issues were developing a rhetoric of their own and conjoined with time-honored Puritan notions of calling and of election. No less an authority than Richard Baxter, whose work Dickinson recommended to Austin on at least one occasion (L 110), asserted that in refusing an opportunity to acquire wealth "you cross one of the ends of your calling, and you refuse to be God's steward, and to accept His gifts, and use them for Him when He requireth it: you may labour to be rich for God, though not for flesh and sin." From the time of Cotton Mather's endorsement of calling, Christian piety had been given a place in the world of business. "Prosperity, being first commended for its underlying moral qualities or as evidence of divine favor," writes Ralph Perry, came finally to be "commended in itself."[6]

This tendency became still more pronounced through the nineteenth century. Marvin Meyers, in *The Jacksonian Persuasion*, traces how an expanding economy and political struggles over its management gave rise to a public discourse defending the pursuit of wealth in moral terms. "Prosperity and poverty [were] conceived as fixed states of reward and punishment, between which people move according to personal traits: their habits, their virtues and vices." Thus, Thomas Sedgwick, in his *Public and Private Economy*, declared that the "virtue, wisdom, and character" of every individual was measured by his economic performance.[7]

Such interfusing of spiritual with material terms extended not only into the marketplace but into the pulpit. Emerson deplored sermons that proposed the rewards in the next life to consist of "bank-stock and doubloons, venison and champagne."[8] Within the pulpit world, however, the concept of exchange was not inherently alien. Among the basic tenets of American Calvinism was the idea of covenant, according to which "man has not only been in relation to God as creature to Creator, but more definitely through a succession of explicit agreements or contracts, as between two partners in a business enterprise." After Adam's failure to fulfill the terms of this partnership, the contract was renewed under Christ as a covenant of grace. In return for faith in Christ on man's part, God for his part pledges to redeem man and to glorify him. The conception is a legal one: God delivers "to man a signed and sealed bond" with Christ as "surety."[9]

Dickinson does not hesitate to adopt what she calls the "pretty ways of Covenant" (P 944) for her own purposes:

I asked no other thing—
No other—was denied—
I offered Being—for it—
The Mighty Merchant sneered—   [P 621]

Even with "Being" proffered, the omnipotent Merchant declines the transaction. In the context of the Puritan covenant of Grace, such incidental poems emerge as theological statements:

I gave myself to Him—
And took Himself, for Pay,
The solemn contract of a Life
Was ratified this way—

The Wealth might disappoint—
Myself a poorer prove
Than this great Purchaser suspect,
The Daily Own—of Love

Depreciate the Vision—
But till the Merchant buy—
Still Fable—in the Isles of Spice—
The subtle Cargoes—lie—

At least—'tis Mutual—Risk—
Some—found it—Mutual Gain—
Sweet Debt of Life—Each Night to owe—
Insolvent—every Noon—   [P 580]

The poem opens with an assertion of a ratified contract. Each succeeding stanza, however, recants on this initial assertion. In the second stanza, the poet questions both the value of "Wealth" to be received and the mutual understanding on which an exchange must be based. The "great Purchaser" may not have accurately estimated his partner, for the poet may not be willing to meet the demands of the Merchant. She may be unwilling to pledge to him her "Daily Own—of Love," in comparison with which, in any case, the "Vision" of heaven is depreciated. The whole transaction, as the third stanza then declares, remains provisional. It is not certain that the Merchant will buy; the "subtle Cargo" to be negotiated is a "Fable" which may not even materialize. The last stanza finally, though subtly, dissolves the whole proceeding. A "Mutual Gain" has been progressively questioned. Only the "Mutual Risk" is certain, and this seems too great to the poet to warrant completion of the contract. The debt, for uncertain commodities, is, the poem implies, never repaid. Owed at night, at noon it is insolvent.

Dickinson hence denies the validity of a contract posed in rhetoric reminiscent of that between man and God. She suspects its terms, its promises, and its Transactor. Heaven's, she writes elsewhere, is a "Constancy with a Proviso" (P 1357). And even should God agree to terms and fulfill them, there is no guarantee that the contract would be equitable. The "market price" for the poet's "Being's worth" is but "A single Dram of Heaven" (P 1725)—a great deal to ask in return for what may prove little. There is a sense that Dickinson distrusts God's terms of exchange and the values he offers.

From a suspicion that the divine may default in its obligations to the human, Dickinson proceeds to a suspicion that the human and divine are in opposition. Each constitutes a separate order of existence, with no common terms between them. The supposed compensations of the other world do not address the conditions they are meant to compensate. At the same time, the divine makes innumerable demands on the human, for which the return is inadequate or inappropriate. Demands issuing from such a removed sphere do not complement, but in fact, conflict with the earthly order. What heaven requires comes directly to contradict the terms and requirements of the phenomenal world.

This conflict erupts as a fundamental discord between Dickinson and God. It informed her earliest religious rebellion. Writing to Abiah Root at the age of sixteen, she explained her resistance to the call of Christ: "I have perfect confidence in God and his promises, and yet I know not why, I feel that the world holds a predominant place in my affections" (L 13). A sense that the demands of heaven are greater than she can fulfill becomes, in later letters, a sense that they are greater than she should fulfill. "I wonder often how the love of Christ is done—when that below holds so" (L 262). There is an opposition between the love she feels for the world she knows and the love due the unknown world. The claims of the latter seem a direct threat to the claims of the former, until Dickinson asks, "Is God love's Adversary?" (L 792).

Thus, instead of seeing the world of heaven as reward, justification, or sanction for earthly life, Dickinson comes to see it as a threat to earthly life. "The Maker's cordial visage," she writes, is shunned "Like an adversity" (P 1718). The afterworld is to be avoided rather than embraced:

> Some Wretched creature, savior take
> Who would exult to die
> And leave for thy sweet mercy's sake
> Another Hour to me.   [P 1111]

Dickinson rejects the savior's salvation and turns the mercy of clerical discourse against its own purposes. She seeks distance from the source of love rather than union with it. What emerges is a sharp divergence between the earthly and heavenly stances. From life's standpoint, heaven is something to be shunned. Conversely, heaven's viewpoint undermines that of earth:

> No Other can reduce
> Our mortal Consequence
> Like the remembering it be nought
> A Period from hence
> But Contemplation for
> Contemporaneous Nought
> Our Single Competition
> Jehovah's Estimate.   [P 982]

Projecting forward to a retrospect from immortality reduces this world to a "nought." The poet tries to adopt this heavenly assessment while still in the mortal world. She contemplates a "Nought" contemporaneous with her mortal state, but she does so only to reassert a human perspective in opposition to the immortal one. For this is not how she sees her world. It is rather a vision in competition with her own. The poem thus shifts to a divine perspective, attempts to apply its standards while within the human sphere, and then rejects this proleptic retrospective. "Jehovah's Estimate" is not compatible with the estimate of mortality. It belittles the mortal world. It represents a viewpoint that denies the stature and value of earthly existence.

The two viewpoints are not merely different. They so oppose each other as to seem mutually exclusive. Acceptance of one entails denial of the other. Dickinson proceeds from this complaint to several statements. She asserts that it is unjust to apply divine standards to earthly conditions:

> Not what We did, shall be the test
> When Act and Will are done
> But what Our Lord infers We would
> Had We diviner been—   [P 823]

God, however, applies his standards. And since they are contrary to and exclusive of this world, conformity to them entails a detachment from the earth. Sacrifices are requisite, not only for their consequent reward, but because allegiance to God seems to preclude an allegiance to this world. From suspicions of heaven's existence and value, Dickinson finally comes to suspect its demands and the whole scheme in which attainment of the world to come is predicated upon denial of and detachment from this world:

> For Death—or rather
> For the Things 'twould buy
> This—put away
> Life's Opportunity—
>
> The Things that Death will buy
> Are Room—
> Escape from Circumstances—
> And a Name—

With Gifts of Life
How Death's Gifts may compare—
We know not—
For the Rates—lie Here—   [P 382]

Immortality offers infinitude: "Room." It obviates the contingent
and the accidental: "Escape from Circumstances." It constitutes absolute and unchanging identity: "Name." It is thus the antithesis of
the least pleasing aspects of the mortal condition and represents a
refuge from them. At the same time, it entails the loss of this world. In
exchange for the promise of immortality, we must sacrifice "Life's
Opportunity." At such cost, it may not be worth procuring, and such
sacrifice may not only be excessive but pointless: "With Gifts of
Life / How Death's Gifts may compare— / We know not." The whole
sacrifice is based on an unknown, against whose worth the poet
asserts the worth of what she has: "the Rates lie Here." The poem
concludes with an affirmation of the "Gifts of Life" and a refusal to
displace them for projected "Gifts."

Dickinson's objections to orthodox theology here are strangely reminiscent of objections raised by another writer, whose critique of
theology is more overtly systematic and more polemical than her
own:

> The true world has been constructed out of contradiction to the actual
> world. . . . The true world: unattainable, indemonstrable, unpromisa-
> ble: but the very thought of it—a consolation, an obligation, an impera-
> tive. . . . The true world? unattainable? At any rate, unattained. And
> being unattained, also unknown. Consequently, not consoling, redeem-
> ing, or obligatory. How could something unknown obligate us?[10]

Friedrich Nietzsche's attack on the notion of a transcendent world as
the "true world" and his questions about its supposed relation to
phenomenal reality encapsulate Dickinson's argument in "For
Death." Imagined as "Room— / Escape from Circumstances— /
And a Name," the afterlife is "constructed out of contradiction to the
actual world." How "Death's Gifts" may compare to those of life,
writes Dickinson, "We know not," for the other world is, as Nietzsche
states, undemonstrable, unattained, unknown. The necessity to "Put
away Life's Opportunity" for it becomes questionable. As Nietzsche

asks, "How could something unknown obligate us?" Both agree on the epistemological problem presented by an otherworld.

Both agree with regard to the axiological problems presented by an otherworld as well. Indeed, Dickinson's discontent with an otherworld as conflicting with and demanding this world's sacrifice is essentially similar to Nietzsche's critique of metaphysical systems. Like Dickinson, Nietzsche objects to placing the meaning of earthly existence in a world separate from it so that "we cannot reach the sphere in which we have placed our values."[11] The sphere of values becomes extramundane, and this determines our attitude toward the mundane world as a negative one. We come to "look at reality from a superior vantage point," from which "the concept of nature" comes to be seen as "the opposite of God." And nature is made a "synonym for the reprehensible."[12] For the sake of a higher reality, we are then supposed to deny the natural world:

> To become perfect, [man] was advised to draw in his senses, turtle fashion, to cease all intercourse with earthly things, to shed his mortal shroud: then his essence would remain, the "pure spirit."[13]

> The world becomes for him overfull of things that must be hated and eternally combatted. . . . And so he ends, quite reasonably, by considering nature evil, mankind corrupt, goodness an act of grace (that is, impossible for man). In summa: he denies life.[14]

Emily Dickinson was not a philosopher and never systematized her religious critique. Persistent in her poetry, however, is a sense of contradiction between phenomenal and transcendent realities such as Nietzsche describes:

> I had some things that I called mine—
> And God, that he called his,
> Till, recently a rival Claim
> Disturbed these amities.   [P 116]

Things of God come to oppose things of man. For Dickinson, as for Nietzsche, the division has led to a system of rival claims. Nietzsche, however, proceeds from this to denounce heaven as a fiction and to attempt to construct a system of values based on other premises entirely. Dickinson's responses to the questions she raises are never so definitive. The framework provided by heaven, with all its problematic demands, continues to define Dickinson's conceptual system. She does not dismiss the divine imperatives, but turns her attention toward examining what seems to her their injustice, toward asserting her own claims against them.

In the combat that ensues, the value of earth becomes the first contested point. And Dickinson, in one strategy, will insist on the supremacy of the life she has over an "Immortality" which remains "only inferential" (L 942). However infinite is "The Life that we shall see," she concludes that "the smallest Human Heart's extent / Reduces it to none" (P 1162). Earthly love is thus lauded over heavenly, the "mysteries of human nature" over the "mysteries of redemption: for the infinite we only suppose, while we see the finite" (L 389). Embracing her palpable world is preferable to denouncing it for the impalpable.

The triviality of earthly things which a heavenly perspective imposes she likewise contests:

> The worthlessness of Earthly things
> The Sermon is that Nature Sings—
> And then—enforces their delight
> Till Zion is inordinate—   [P 1373][15]

Zion she finds limitlessly in the natural world, precluding any longing for a heavenly Jerusalem. It provides its own arguments against the pulpit wisdom that would devalue it. For the evidence that would support nature's lack speaks instead in its favor. In view of earth's attractions, heaven's injunctions can be ignored: "Is not 'Lead us not into Temptation' an involuntary plea under circumstances so gorgeous?" (L 951).

There is, however, a hint of retraction even in these dictums against earthly worthlessness. It is "Nature" herself who provides the "Sermon" warning against its own value. Its elevation must disregard those faults of which Dickinson, in spite of her efforts, remains cognizant. The pain entailed in nature's inconsistency and mutability cannot be long ignored. At times, and even against the continued consciousness of defect, this world will be lauded as superior:

There is a June when Corn is cut
And Roses in the Seed—
A Summer briefer than the first
But tenderer indeed

As should a Face supposed the Grave's
Emerge a single Noon
In the Vermilion that it wore
Affect us, and return—

Two Seasons, it is said, exist—
The Summer of the Just,
And this of Ours, diversified
With Prospect, and with Frost—

May not our Second with its First
So infinite compare
That We but recollect the one
The other to prefer?   [P 930]

Nature continues as its own advocate. Its transitory aspect is immediately conceded, but this is held up as a virtue. The second, Indian
"summer" of harvest or of planting, which forms the subject of another poem (P 1422), is confessedly briefer than the actual June. But
in spite of—and even because of—such brevity, it is "tenderer." This
image of nature then serves as proof to support the poem's subsequent abstraction. Earthly seasons are conditioned by time and hence
are diversified by a "Prospect" which admits its own incompletion in
looking forward to some future fulfillment and by a "Frost" which at
times disappoints its expectations. Still, the poet raises the temporal
summer over that of "the Just," unbounded as this may be by such
conditions, and where, instead, as Isaac Watts concurs, "Everlasting
spring abides / and never withering flowers" (626). The notion of
infinity is even claimed for the earthly.

   Without denying the fact of time, the poet here prefers it to the
immutable. Yet again, there is some hesitation. The confusing syntax
of the final stanza makes it at first unclear which sphere is in fact
preferred. The "Second" season suggests, in itself, that which will
follow a prior one—a second world that will succeed this present one.
But the earthly season has been named in the third stanza as "this of

114

Ours." It is this "Our" season, named second, that is given preference in the final verse. The decision does go to earth, not to heaven. But the syntactic skirmish registers some contrary impulse.

More contrary still is the image presented in the second stanza. The poem's opening proposes a natural image as evidence for the superiority of what may be fleeting. But the second stanza, which is offered as a further instance of such superiority, is highly unnatural. The return of the dead from the grave imagined here is a triumph over nature and mortality and represents a defeat of the temporal conditions the poem seeks to sanction. The acceptance of temporal bounds is therefore undercut rather than supported by this supposed example of time's merits. Dickinson would, it is clear, argue for the ascendancy of this world. But she finds it difficult to set aside her continuing sense of its mortal limitations.

What she would ultimately prefer instead is the world she indirectly projects in this poem: one immanent and palpable, but without loss. She confesses herself to feel more at home with flowers than with saints (L 417); she attests that Christ himself "was uncontented till he had been human" (L 519). Even aspects of the earthly experience that are rooted in temporality are cherished if only they endured. To Mrs. Henry Hills, she wrote: "I think heaven will not be as good as earth, unless it bring with it that sweet power to remember, which is the Staple of Heaven—here. How can we thank each other, when omnipotent?" (L 623). There seems a harshness to perfection. When all time is one, there is no room for memory. When everyone has all and does all, there is no room for mutual exchange: "A Letter is a joy of Earth—it is denied the Gods" (L 963). The terms of human love, with its gentleness and sympathy, seem precluded by a suprahuman condition. It is not merely that heaven is underimagined, as Wallace Stevens suggests, but that aspects of its experience seem inherently flawed. Only the fact that remembering often means having irrevocably lost what is no longer present renders the world and time bitter.

Apotheosis of nature therefore depends upon granting it those qualities that seem to make heaven desirable; having them would indeed be the superior state. This, however, is not the case; and nature ultimately remains in Dickinson's work insufficient, while heaven persists as a vital concept, if only by contrast. But given the fact that the benefits of mortal existence seem exclusive of those of immortality, Dickinson will aggressively assail the latter in the name of the former. "To be willing the Kingdom of Heaven invade our own," she writes, "requires years of sorrow."[16] Though the "Just" themselves were to "offer a Reward," she will refuse her "Booty" to the God who would rob her of it (P 900). "Back from the cordial Grave" she will drag those near her and will ward off that divine "spacious arm . . . That none can understand" (P 1625). Present possession will be vociferously defended against incursion. She will not relinquish what she has for what may be beyond.

She will, instead, protest what is denied to earth and what makes heaven enviable—circumstances the poet finds far from innocent. The envy extends in both directions and is a source of all that detracts from earthly happiness. It is indeed a "Jealous God" who "cannot bear to see" the human companionship in which omnipotent heaven cannot share (P 1719). The design of creation seems directed toward keeping heaven's advantage over creatures willfully—even maliciously—made mortal. This world, "were it not riddled by partings," would be "too divine" (L 860). Always "An Obstacle is given . . . Lest this be Heaven indeed" (P 1043).

In Dickinson's ironic argument, such obstacles constitute the best evidence of God's existence, if not of his goodness:

> Immortal is an ample word
> When what we need is by
> But when it leaves us for a time
> 'Tis a necessity.
>
> Of Heaven above the firmest proof
> We fundamental know
> Except for its marauding Hand
> It had been Heaven below.   [P 1205]

This profession of satiric theism presents a God whom the poet cannot praise, but she cannot banish him either. Against the claims of heaven she asserts an earth which would itself be paradise were it not for mortality. But death, which makes us turn toward heaven, is itself due to heavenly interference and is, therefore, also a severe indictment of God. In this circular posing of force against itself, the hand of heaven is affirmed a "fundamental" knowledge—but that hand is a thief and pillager. The assertion of earthly life as edenic becomes a form of criticism against heaven's intrusions. But that criticism conversely asserts the reality of heaven and constitutes its "proof."

Such blasphemy is, in Dickinson, more than a conceptual position. It is a linguistic mode with poetic constructions and stances peculiar to it. Much of Dickinson's religious critique in fact assumes a blasphemous form. Overt blasphemy, in turn, is rooted in critique and reiterates, aggressively, her criticisms while remaining directed heavenward. In rhetorical terms, her forms continue to be those of appeal, which, however, question their own possibility. They comprise a construction of reciprocal contesting/attesting elements:

Of God we ask one favor
That we may be forgiven—
For what, he is presumed to know—
The Crime, from us, is hidden—

Immured the whole of Life
Within a magic Prison
We reprimand the Happiness
That too competes with Heaven.   [P 1601]

This blasphemous outburst resumes Dickinson's several points of metaphysical critique. Suing for forgiveness becomes accusation. We plead before an uncertain throne "presumed to know" laws which are unclear to us but by which we are nonetheless judged. Unclear as well is the validity of those laws. "The Crime, from us, is hidden" both because the laws are obscure and because they judge us criminal when we are not so. God insists that "We reprimand the Happiness" we have because it will qualify our desire to forgo life in heaven's name. Our crime is in fact attachment to the world.

But the poet protests that world and heaven need compete. She protests that attachment to this world is a sin necessitating absolution or that absolution need be the basis of the human relation to the divine. Nietzsche had assailed the scheme in which "the concept of punishment and the concept of sin [are] at the heart of the interpretation of existence."[17] Dickinson does so as well.

The critique presented here is nevertheless presented as appeal.

117

"Of God we ask" is a gesture of invocation. It is an attempt to penetrate to the divine, although it is so through aggression. And, in this, it is very close to prayer. As an assault on divine distance, it is an effort to bridge that distance and to reach God, if only to admonish him. There is a constant tension between affirmation and denial, as Dickinson condemns God but in doing so invokes him. This tension is felt in her pervasive use of hymnal meters for blasphemous purposes; in her formulations of accusation as petition; in her sudden inversions of religious topoi to condemn religious dicta. "Going to Heaven!" she writes, but adds, "I'm glad I don't believe it" (P 79). "Heavenly Father," she prays, but does so to attest "thine own Duplicity" (P 1461). This impulse in herself she will sometimes mock: "We pray to [God], and He answers 'No.' Then we pray to Him to rescind the 'no,' and He don't answer at all, yet 'Seek and ye shall find' is the boon of faith" (L 830). Irony controls her utterance, which remains nonetheless a religious form. Hers here are structures of inverted appeal to heaven, protesting heaven's indifference to appeal. Blasphemy emerges as a mode of prayer.

Blasphemy-as-prayer merges, in Dickinson's work, with a corresponding mode, that of prayer-as-blasphemy. In this mode, the desire to overcome the gap between human and divine love implicit in her blasphemous assaults becomes explicit. Such poems declare her full need for the divine and show her blasphemies to be a response to frustration of that need. If blasphemy-as-prayer opens with an ironic appeal and concludes with a direct attack, prayer-as-blasphemy opens with a direct appeal and concludes with its ironic and agonized defeat. The form can emerge under strange guises and with gentle acrimony. A poem purporting to be of love may be the vehicle of such meek bitterness:

> I got so I could take his name—
> Without—Tremendous gain—
> That Stop-sensation—on my Soul—
> And Thunder—in the Room—
>
> I got so I could walk across
> That Angle in the floor,
> Where he turned so, and I turned—how—
> And all our Sinew tore—

I got so I could stir the Box—
In which his letters grew
Without that forcing, in my breath—
As Staples—driven through—

Could dimly recollect a Grace—
I think, they call it "God"—
Renowned to ease Extremity—
When Formula, had failed—

And shape my Hands—
Petition's way,
Tho' ignorant of a word
That Ordination—utters—

My Business, with the Cloud,
If any Power behind it, be,
Not subject to Despair—
It care, in some remoter way,
For so minute affair
As Misery—
Itself, too vast, for interrupting—more—   [P 293]

Whether an actual lover is or is not the subject of this poem—and
the scene of a quarrel in the poet's chamber clearly could not have
occurred—the tearing asunder so movingly recorded here is made
into an image of troubled intercourse with love's Source—and may
indeed reflect this image. The opening "take his name" at least suggests a Biblical prototype for this temporal discord. And the poem's
increasingly central figure of discourse—first temporal and then sacred—is consonant with Dickinson's own preoccupation, in form and
as subject, with an utterance that confronts God.

The question of discourse is subtly posed. In the temporal stanzas,
it is a matter of names and of letters—of the box which holds written
words and of the staples which could join together, but which instead
sunder. Dickinson's relationships were highly epistolary; her chronic
consciousness of loss had often led her to regard her letter box as a
coffin for dead love: as she writes, "If it is finished, tell me, and I will
raise the lid to my Box of Phantoms and lay one more love in" (L 177).
In the moment of extreme distress this would incur, she attempts

another address: to heaven for solace, adopting the stance of prayer. The approach is humbly made; the poet confesses her need and her longing. The ensuing disappointment, it is true, is heralded even here in her diction. She only "dimly" recalls a grace of whose very name she is unsure. But this skepticism is carefully tempered by the fact of her "Extremity." She may be incredulous of the "Formula" proposed by clergymen, but she tries to frame her own entreaty. The movement from concern with temporal interlocutor to a divine one is hesitant, but could succeed and assuage her earlier disappointment.

Instead, it is shown to be not a complementary experience but a repetitive one. The failed love on earth is not made whole. It is re-enacted by a failed heavenly love. The response from above is as meager as that which the poet has already received. Clark Griffith's argument seems relevant here, that Dickinson's love poetry reflects a betrayal not by a corporeal lover but by all the men Dickinson did love: her father, her brother, and God.[18] The final stanza, in any event, turns on the relation between the world below and that above—with the emphasis on the latter. Against her immediate need she poses "some remoter care" of heaven. And if from heaven's point of view her own acute misery seems minute, the minute here reduces what is great: a reduction that reproaches divine indifference.

That reproach remains oblique. It is evinced in the tension of the contrast between earth and heaven, and in the introduction of a subjunctive mood:

> My Business, with the Cloud,
> If any power behind it, be
> Not subject to despair
> It care in some remoter way
> As Misery—
> Itself, too vast, for interrupting—more—

Heaven becomes a hypothetical power, further qualified by its possible subjection to despair—although syntactic ambiguity leaves open whether this qualified power is subject to the poet's despair or is itself despairing.[19] The poet's involvement with it becomes increasingly indefinite. Even the remote care is made hypothesis. And the return to declarative utterance at the poem's conclusion finally displaces this tenuous intercourse with a discourse both certain and overwhelming: the articulation of misery.

The poem is thus composed of different modes of discourse struggling for completion and against interruption. Failed intercourse with a beloved becomes a type of failed intercourse with God. The poet is finally left with only her own address, uninterrupted in one sense but incomplete in another in its lack of any auditor. Her prayer has, through successive syntactic disguises, been defeated and become blasphemous. From petition it becomes a description of utterance turned back upon itself.

Prayer, in this way, becomes an avenue of defiance. Its speech act is appropriated for contrary purposes. This pattern is repeatedly enacted. "Just Once! Oh least Request" becomes a fear that the "God of Flint" will refuse even "So small a Grace" (P 1076). Attempts at prayer, meeting with refusal, become complaints: "Of Course—I prayed— / And did God care?" (P 376), she writes. "There comes an hour . . . When the long interceding lips / Perceive that prayer is vain" (P 1751). Petition becomes aggressive, while aggression remains a mode of supplication:

Prayer is the little implement
Through which Men reach
Where Presence—is denied them.
They fling their Speech

By means of it—in God's Ear—
If then He hear—
This sums the Apparatus
Comprised in Prayer—   [P 437]

Through prayer men "fling their Speech" toward a "Presence" which this poem does not expect to reach. And what prayer does accomplish remains unstated. "By means of it" is interrupted by the poet's underlying doubt: "If then He hear." The little implement is shown to be unequal to its task. But its task is also revealed. Dickinson accepts the mediatory function of language. Through it, she still strives toward an interaction with heaven. Whether in supplicating contention or in contending supplication, she still gropes toward the realm of Presence and does so as a linguistic act.

Dickinson's poetic utterance thus entails modes of discourse that contend against their own protests but undercut the hope of which they also speak. The balance between these contraposing elements can accordingly shift from accusatory prayer to a suspended accusation which retains its patience, even in the face of disappointment. In this process, attention finally comes to focus upon the speech act which is granted a special place as the field of contending forces. The blasphemy that protests divine indifference and reaches toward God in negative terms forms the basis out of which Dickinson gropes toward a language that can be affirmative. The need for mediation remains strong. Language retains its mediatory function. And even while expressing fear at its failure to mediate, Dickinson maintains her hope that it will succeed:

> I've none to tell me to but Thee
> So when Thou failest, nobody.
> It was a little tie—
> It just held Two, nor those it held
> Since Somewhere thy sweet Face has spilled
> Beyond my Boundary—
>
> If things were opposite—and Me
> And Me it were—that ebbed from Thee
> On some unanswering Shore—
> Would'st Thou seek so—just say
> That I the Answer may pursue
> Unto the lips it eddied through—
> So—overtaking Thee—   [P 881]

Dickinson addresses herself to God in an act that defines both her conceived relation to him and her conception of language in that relation. God is called on to be her auditor, her communicant. And language is the "tie" that binds them together. But this tie has been disrupted. The bond holding the two together no longer holds them. The divine face has "spilled / Beyond my Boundary." Infinitude has become a barrier, and God fails her as an interlocutor. The linguistic tie to him has broken.

But it has not therefore been discarded. The poet reaffirms her direction as toward God. He has, like a receding tide, ebbed to an "unanswering Shore." But from her own shore, the poet continues to await an answer. She requests that, through speech, he turn toward her, just as she, through speech, seeks for him: "Just say." This speech would then provide the bridge to him for which she longs. She could pursue this answer to the "lips" which would remain distant, but which would no longer be inaccessible.

"Overtaking" God becomes possible in this poem through the reversal of direction imaged in the tides. In the first stanza, the poet faces toward an infinitude which her language cannot reach. As long as movement occurs only from the finite toward the infinite, the latter remains inaccessible. In the second stanza, the movement is instead from the infinite toward the finite. Dickinson's experience of heaven's disjunction from earth had been consistently founded on her sense that the other world, as the focus of meaning, led to a denial of this one. If the focus could instead be shifted to this world, such that the finite would not be subsumed into the infinite, but rather, the infinite would be brought into the finite, the gap between the two could be overcome. In "I've none to tell me to," this reorientation is proposed. The poet requests that God, instead of remaining self-enclosed beyond the world, himself turn toward the earth as a returning tide and, even more, as an answering voice. His voice would then no longer be entirely transcendent, and to hear it, one would not need to transcend the earth. It would infuse the finite world and be experienced therein.

Dickinson is here reaching toward the only resolution possible to her blasphemous stance: that of a responsive heaven, whose power and value can be experienced in terms of temporal phenomena. In such a resolution, both terms of her blasphemous structure would be retained. The traditional heaven in its relation to earth would not be affirmed; but the earth without some transcendent principle would also be denied. A stark redefinition of the interchange between both heaven and earth would instead be necessary, in what approaches an alternative metaphysic. Heaven would not be a realm that displaces the earth as its end and as the locus of its meaning, reducing finite experience to mere vestibule. Instead, the order instituted by heaven would be felt within a coherent temporal world invested with significance. What is implied is a reorientation of divine and human interaction, making transcendent activity effective within the processes of the temporal world.

In attempting to describe this redefined relation, Dickinson speaks of sanctifying the earth, of a present salvation, of an eternity felt within time. "While the Clergyman tells Father and Vinnie that 'this Corruptible shall put on Incorruption'—it has already done so and they go defrauded" (L 391), she writes. "You have the most triumphant Face out of Paradise—probably because you are there constantly, instead of ultimately" (L 489). In her poems she speaks of summer as a "Sacrament" in whose "sacred emblems" she partakes (P 130). "Forever—is composed of Nows" and can be attested "From this—experienced Here" (P 624).

Such expressions suggest, but must be distinguished from, "Transcendentalist identification of truth or divinity with symbolic nature," as Charles Anderson notes. "Emily Dickinson did not pretend to read ultimate meanings in nature, human or divine, either in terms of Butler's *Analogy* or Emerson's Correspondences." But Anderson then proposes that heaven becomes for Dickinson "an inner truth of nature . . . intuited in the mind,"[20] a position also Emersonian and ultimately not Dickinson's. Dickinson is certainly confronting the metaphysical imbalance that had become a crisis in the work of her contemporaries, Emerson among them, and continues as one for her successors. Her attempts at resolution, however, must be situated and defined against those who would resolve tensions between heaven and earth at the expense of either.

Melville, as his diatribe on chronometrical and horological time shows, had come to suspect an utter disjunction between the spheres of heaven and earth:

> Though earthly wisdom of man may be heavenly folly to God; so also, conversely, is the heavenly wisdom of God earthly folly to man. . . . Whatever other worlds God may be Lord of, He is not the Lord of this; for else this world would seem to give the lie to Him; so utterly repugnant seem its ways to the instinctively known ways of Heaven.[21]

This vociferous denial of any conceivable concordance between this world and the next was presumably prompted by transcendentalist assertions of evident concord. Emerson, himself troubled by living in a "transition period, when the old faiths which comforted nations, and not only so but made nations, seem to have spent their force," seemed to overcome the distinctions between transcendence and immanence by asserting their near equation. Thus he calls the world a "temple" and declares that nature "certifying the supernatural" is to be worshipped with "sincere rites," that there is an ineffable "union of man and God in every act of the soul."[22]

Emerson's arguments may indirectly hint time's mutability to have been for him, as it was for Dickinson, problematic. He persistently gainsays its power—insisting that man is capable of "abolishing" it and assuring that "the least activity of the intellectual powers redeems us in a degree from the influences of time." The volume of his denial suggests the degree of concern; to defend against the negative effects of time, Emerson will rise to its praise. In "Circles" he pronounces the universe to be "fluid and volatile"—and gives this as evidence of, and inspiration for, a creative energy and an ever-expanding soul: "The heart refuses to be imprisoned; in its first and narrowest pulses it already tends outward with a vast force and to immense and innumerable expansions."[23] But this is not so much a reconciliation between the mutable and immutable as a blurring of distinctions. It is, in one sense, to claim for the temporal the power of the supramundane. In another sense, it subserves the temporal to an eternal model and, rather than investing time with significance, abolishes its limits. Eternity finally remains the significant sphere. Though Emerson may write in "Considerations by the Way" that "Nature is upheld by antagonism," he also writes that "the first fact that strikes us is our delight in permanence. All great natures are lovers of stability and permanence, as the type of the Eternal."[24] Emerson's system remains dualistic, as Margaret Homans points out:

> Despite the transparency between self and world that Emerson prophecies, and the infinitude of his individual man, his philosophic universe depends on dualism as much as any in tradition, [including] a dichotomy between matter and spirit, among others, and from Dickinson's point of view there cannot have been much difference between parodier and parodied.[25]

If, in his essay on Montaigne, Emerson urges that men "look for the permanent in the mutable and fleeting," he then grounds such permanence in an essentially immutable "world-spirit" and in a faith that whatever passes here will emerge more truly on "another sea."[26] Consecration of the temporal remains based on a prior conception and apotheosis of the eternal.

The course that Dickinson pursues is at once less progressive and more radical. To her, neither earth nor self, but only God, is divine; but the divine activity becomes focused within the immanent world. This is implied when she writes that "to have been immortal transcends to become so" (L 441). The value of immortality most inheres in its effects on mortals who, like herself in one poem, "instead of going to Heav'n, at last" are "going, all along" (P 324). Salvation is not relegated to the other world but becomes an active principle in this one: "The Province of the Saved / Should be the Art / To save" (P 539). And to sanctify the earth would not be to establish it as heaven but to experience within it "the Heaven—unexpected come" (P 513). Dickinson thus strives neither to exclude nor to appropriate, but to realize heaven as a felt presence during this life. She strives to reorient the emphasis from the afterworld to the present one and to redefine their relation so that transcendence would not be denied nor would this world be denied for it. Its power would be accessible within the temporal world.

Emerson, in "Circles," had named his experience of endlessly outward expansion a "self-evolving circle" for which there "is no outside, no inclosing wall, no circumference." Dickinson, no doubt adopting his term, had likewise announced "Circumference" to be her special "Business" (L 268). As Charles Anderson warns when discussing the term, "the meanings it carries are not always consistent." But he associates it with consciousness extended to the farthest limit, as does Alfred Gelpi. Both critics refer it, as Emerson had done, to an Augustinian image of God as "a circle of which the center is everywhere and the circumference nowhere."[27] For Anderson, this becomes to Dickinson a center as "the inquiring mind . . . intent upon exploring the whole infinity of the universe that lies before her."[28] For Gelpi, it is the "farthest boundary of human experience." Eternity and God are "the encircling infinity into which the individual may expand in accordance with his inner capacity." Circumference is then the limit that "separates man from God" but is also the point at which the human circle "presses that which was beyond" so that "time transcends time."[29]

Certainly circumference is one of Dickinson's images for a relation between the self and infinity or eternity. She places it "Twixt Firmament above / And Firmament below" (P 1343). It is the boundary "That secures Eternity / From presenting—Here" (P 889). Immortality is a "Circumference without Relief" (P 943). But circumference does more than delineate a border involving the human and the beyond. It suggests a particular interaction at that border and a particular relation between the two realms. And this relation is not, in Dickinson, necessarily one of perfect concordance between them, or of a perfect synecdoche in which the inner circle represents and paradoxically contains the infinite. Such synecdoche had been Emerson's dream, if not his assured reality. In "Self-Reliance" he makes it the basis of an ontology:

> This is the ultimate fact . . . the resolution of all into the ever-blessed One. Self-existence is the attribute of the Supreme Cause, and it constitutes the measure of good by the degree in which it enters into all lower forms. All things real are so by virtue as they contain.

Every being is real to the degree that it contains the whole. This is true of man as well; and Emerson accordingly extends synecdoche from an ontology to a discipline:

> Every true man is a cause, a country, and an age. . . . Thus all concentrates: let us not rove; let us sit at home with the cause. Let us stun and astonish the intruding rabble of men . . . by a simple declaration of the divine fact. Bid the invaders take the shoes from off their feet, for God is here within.[30]

It is tempting to envision Dickinson as a disciple of this Emersonian regimen. Emerson had developed the Puritan emphasis on an inner voice through which the infinite speaks, making the self into an infinite world. And he had secularized the synecdochic paradox which declares the inner life to be greater than the outer one, blurring the distinction between the soul and the divine. Dickinson, too, in her many poems on the self-in-reclusion seems to adopt Emerson's stance, declaring herself a world. But Dickinson, with this as with other dialectical patterns, breaks the synecdoche and dissolves the paradox into unsynthesized antitheses. The retreat into the self as a place for encountering God is at times traced. "On a Columnar Self— / How ample to rely," she declares, and concludes:

> Suffice Us—for a Crowd—
> Ourself—and Rectitude—
> And that Assembly—not far off
> From furthest Spirit—God—   [P 789]

This assertion of the single self as a sufficient whole is touched by irony at the last, where God hovers between acting as the outermost circumference the self can reach or as the furthest limit most removed from it. A similar suggestion of irony intrudes in the conditional *if* of: "The Soul should always stand ajar / That if the Heaven inquire / He will not be obliged to wait" (P 1055). The seemingly univocal poem, "The Soul selects her own Society," involves a more pervasive irony:

> The Soul selects her own Society—
> Then—shuts the Door—
> To her divine Majority—
> Present no more—
>
> Unmoved—she notes the Chariots—pausing—
> At her low Gate—
> Unmoved—an Emperor be kneeling
> Upon her Mat—
>
> I've known her—from an ample nation—
> Choose One—
> Then—close the Valves of her attention—
> Like Stone—   [P 303]

Here we seem to find what we expect from an Emersonian Dickinson: the plenitude of the self, its imperial status, what Clark Griffith describes as an "air of royalty . . . attested to by such marks of complete self-sufficiency as the key verbs in the poem: selects, Unmoved, Choose."[31]. There may be some punning on the electoral process which Dickinson had witnessed in her father's various campaigns for public office, but here the "One" chosen from an ample nation is just herself. That "One" might, like Emerson's or like Whitman's as well, still include all. Dickinson's "divine Majority" can be compared with Whitman's "divine average" of "Starting from Paumonok," where he tells how his "is a song . . . of the One form'd out of all."

But the poem seems to present a process of exclusion rather than of inclusion. Griffith suggests that the chariots and emperor "belong to the secular world, to the pomps and pageantry of life" which the spiritual soul scorns.[32] To Charles Anderson, they "suggest future suitors being rejected because of the chosen One, rather than the lure of society that might distract her from her art." Or, "This One may be God . . . taking precedence over mere mortal Emperors."[33] Both chariots and emperors, however, appear elsewhere in Dickinson's verse in a specifically spiritual sense: as chariots that wait to take the soul to heaven (P 236, P 1053), and as Emperors of other worlds "Who recollected us / If we were true" (P 616). This is clearly the meaning of *Emperor* in what seems another version of "The Soul Selects," but which omits its irony:

> The Soul that hath a Guest
> Doth seldom go abroad—
> Diviner Crowd at Home—
> Obliterate the need—
>
> And Courtesy forbid
> A Host's departure when
> Upon Himself be visiting
> The Emperor of Men—   [P 674]

This soul indeed encompasses a "Diviner Crowd" and meets in its chamber the Divine Emperor. But in "The Soul Selects," this may be the very Emperor who is left to kneel outside. And even selfhood takes on an ominous ring: "Then—close the Valves of her attention— / Like Stone—." The diction recalls the "Hour of Lead" of "After Great Pain" (P 341), the "Paralysis / Done perfecter on stone" of "I've dropped my Brain" (P 1046), the "Boots of Lead" of "I felt a Funeral, in my Brain" (P 280), and other poems of utter fragmentation. The soul here has withdrawn into its own center. But instead of finding there the divine whole or the infinite world, it finds only itself.

Dickinson's is the terrible irony of a Puritan or Emersonian retreat into the soul in search of the divine, only to find herself trapped there. The synecdochic containment of the all in the one and the dialectical paradox of an inner world greater than the outer one are not realized here. The inner is merely inward, the one only one. The container contains only itself. The desired experience of inward infinity gives way to claustrophobia.

The possibility of the self as an entrapping circle is often recorded by Dickinson. Withdrawn into herself, she suddenly senses that she may have locked herself in with an "awful Mate" (P 894). The soul may be an "imperial friend"; but it may be "the most agonizing Spy— / An Enemy—could send" (P 683). "One need not be a Chamber—to be Haunted" (P 670) is more than a well-wrought trope. It is a terrifying nightmare of the self caught within itself. The friendly "Prison" ultimately becomes an image of what is "escapeless" (P 652). Dickinson may have been seeking, as was Emerson, the "highest power of divine moments . . . when these waves of God flow into men . . . moments [which] confer a sort of omnipresence and omnipotence." But she was aware that the synecdoche may fail, as indeed was Emerson: "I own I am gladdened," he wrote, "by beholding in morals that unrestrained inundation of the principle of good into every chink and hole that selfishness has left open."[34] Dickinson often seems the antithetical Emerson, his own submerged ironic voice become dominant. The self may be a godlike infinity, or, claiming all for itself, it may be merely selfish. The self may be infinite, but it may also be a fragmentary trap.

Yet, the yearning toward infinity remains strong in Dickinson, and the term *circumference* does signify her particular hope of a self whose center widens outward toward eternity—under the condition that such expansion is not entirely determined by the activity of the self, with its dangers and limits, but also by the activity of the infinite. Circumference is, in one poem, not only "Possessed" but "Possessing" (P 1620). There is a sense of reciprocal action. It is not that the finite self reaches toward the infinite to transcend time but that the infinite reaches into the finite:

Time feels so vast that were it not
For an Eternity—

I fear me this Circumference
Engross my Finity—

To His exclusion, who prepare
By Processes of Size
For the Stupendous Vision
Of His diameters—   [P 802]

Circumference here does involve distinctions. It is situated at the
outermost boundary of time and the innermost boundary of eternity.
The two are in some sense continuous, although the continuity is as
between spheres which remain separate. The circumference of time,
as its vastest extension, may "Engross" the finite and exclude the
infinite and eternal, asserting a division. Yet eternity, although distinct, is prepared for by the "Processes of size" of earthly experience.
Time itself constitutes a figure for the "Stupendous vision" of infinite
diameters. The one secures the other, not only as a sequence in which
time gives way to eternity, but as a present experience itself governed
by the eternal. And it is the present experience that has precedence.
The poet fears lest "this" temporal sphere alone suffice for her. It is
preeminent in her experience, but that preeminence is then placed in
eternity's service, providing an image for its immensity. The two
terms, then, are distinct but not opposed. They are complementary.
Eternity penetrates through time. It remains a promised vision beyond, but is foremostly a present power directing and orienting the
temporal.

Dickinson repeatedly struggles to express this vision of the supramundane as governing but as presently felt within the earthly world.
The effort involves an attempt to assert the integrity of each sphere,
while marking the exact relation by which each posits and invests the
other. This is, however, a delicate balance to keep. Dickinson would
redefine the interrelation between the terms, so as to portray eternity
as a power in time that nonetheless retains its own ontological status.
At times she sustains the structure that would grant each world its
due. But to do so, she must press against the exclusion which each
term continues to imply with regard to the other, retaining as each
does, for her, its implications determined by traditional metaphysics.

131

She must therefore carefully make her way between an idolatry of earth as the ultimate world as against its devaluation when defined by the supramundane:

> The Heaven vests for Each
> In that small Deity
> It craved the grace to worship
> Some bashful Summer's Day—
>
> Half shrinking from the Glory
> It importuned to see
> Till these faint Tabernacles drop
> In full Eternity—
>
> How imminent the Venture—
> As one should sue a Star—
> For His mean sake to leave the Row
> And entertain Despair—
>
> A Clemency so common—
> We almost cease to fear—
> Enabling the minutest—
> And furthest—to adore—   [P 694]

This poem's opening almost invites a transcendentalist reading. Grace is implored in order to worship the natural world. "Each" one who so pleads is vested by heaven with such grace, making every natural phenomenon like unto a "small Deity." The line between heaven and earth grows indistinct, and the poet seems to greet nature with a religious regard. The second stanza, however, begins to assert distinctions once more, while nonetheless retaining the intimate relation sought in the first. The "Glory" with which earthly things are to be endowed is immediately—and somewhat awesomely—witnessed, but is so as a vision of that "full Eternity" yet to come. Earth is not itself the object of worship, but a tabernacle for worship of the divine. It intimates with its own the transcendent glory that remains the source of grace and the highest vision. Thus earth does not accede to heavenly status, but opens a vision to it. And heaven in turn invests the earth with glory.

This is a reconciliation between earthly and heavenly claims which

Dickinson seeks and which Emerson had sought as well. The difference between the two writers is one only of balance between the terms; and Dickinson's own difficulty in retaining her sense of the concurrent but mutually reinforcing claims of each is manifested in the poem's final stanzas. These, if they do not retract, at least qualify the reconciliation by demonstrating its difficulties and even its inconsistencies. The "Venture," Dickinson begins, is "imminent." But her image of its ready fulfillment is something radical. The request for heavenly vestiture of earth is likened to one asking a star to descend from its own heavenly "Row" for the "mean sake" of mortal man. This image may express the greatness of the gift sought, emphasizing the sovereignty of heaven and its inestimable charity in answering man's suit. It may, however, suggest the impossibility of her hopes' fulfillment, that any star would so desert its place above for the sake of those below. The gap between them may be too great. Reconciliation is an illusory desire. The stanza ultimately sustains both senses. The "Despair" that is entertained may be that of heaven and especially of Christ, who willingly enters the human sphere and takes on its burdens. Or it may be that of mortal man, who cannot hope for such condescension.

The poem thus becomes a double text working at cross-purposes with itself. It at once declares the "Clemency" of heavenly response to be common and then hastens to add that the fears this clemency will be withheld are only "almost" silenced. The seemingly secure final assurance, which announces the prayer to have been answered and exactly describes the desired harmony between the near and far, the immanent and transcendent, emerges as supposition. Dickinson wishes to adore the "minutest and furthest" in a continuity and reciprocity with each other. But this state proves insecure. The reciprocity may be contrapuntal. The adoration in one sphere may not admit adoration in the other.

Such mutually contesting but indispensable elements characteristically structure Dickinson's poetic acts. Her attempts to reconceive the relation between the metaphysical and physical spheres finally founder in her continued consciousness of the contradictory aspects of each. She is left with these contradictions and can neither escape nor overcome them, but can only protest them in defiant, defeated, or accusatory prayer:

> You left me—Sire—two Legacies—
> A Legacy of Love
> A Heavenly Father would suffice
> Had He the offer of—
>
> You left me Boundaries of Pain—
> Capacious as the Sea—
> Between Eternity and Time—
> Your Consciousness—and Me—   [P 644]

Heavenly love is staked against its absence. The opposing senses of divine care willed to and possessed by man, and of the tenuous nature of that legacy, are both expressed. But the poem, in its imagery, its diction, and its syntax, speaks more of default than of fulfilled promise. The love of a Heavenly Father would suffice, but its "offer" is conditional. The sea, whose "Verge" is so often a figure for eternity's penetration into time,[35] here represents unbounded distance between the two.

Far more certain than the first is the second legacy of disjunction, disengagement, and indifference dividing the two spheres. Nonetheless, the poem remains an appeal to God. It addresses him as "Sire" and engages him in dialogue. The address promises more petition than the poem actually proffers. The love it cites as its first legacy is, by the poem's second half, engulfed by the sea of pain felt to separate the poet from it. And the poem goes beyond complaint to reproach. But the reproach remains dialogical. Discourse takes place and thus continues at least to reach toward a transcendent interlocutor.

These self-contradictory appeals enact in language what remains Dickinson's contentious stance. "We thank Thee, Oh Father," she writes, "for these strange Minds, that enamor us against Thee" (L 472). The criticisms of orthodox metaphysics, which she shares with other nineteenth-century writers and with writers of the twentieth century, make her unable to embrace the infinite and eternal world of traditional ontology. This sphere, however, remains a determining conception for her. The ensuing clash between her critique of eternity and its continued hold upon her imagination is, in Dickinson's work, finally more than a theological problem. It is a linguistic problem. The strains of denial and assertion generate a poetic mode of inter-contending utterance. And they ultimately inform Dickinson's attitudes toward poetry and toward language. The very possibility of significant linguistic acts is, for Dickinson, implicated by the structure of relation between transcendence and immanence, in which language is a mediator. Through its verbal accusations, Dickinson's work ultimately attempts to assert the very link to heaven, the lack of which it protests. It thus registers contention with, rather than acceptance of, heaven's distance and tries to approach nearer to God by defying his remoteness.

Five

Dickinson's Logos and
the Status of Language

Wisdom is a single thing. It is to understand the Logos by which all
things are steered through all things.
—Heraclitus, *Fragments*

Immediately following the death of her long-time correspondent and
editor of the *Springfield Republican*, Samuel Bowles, Dickinson wrote
his widow:

I am glad if the broken words helped you. I had not hoped so much, I felt
so faint in uttering them, thinking of your great pain. Love makes us
"heavenly" without our trying in the least. 'Tis easier than a Savior—it
does not stay on high and call us to its distance; its low "come unto me"
begins in every place. [L 536]

In this letter, Dickinson places her language into a theological context.
Heavenly words—indeed, the heavenly Word—should administer the
comfort she here offers her bereaved friend. She implies that this
ministry has failed. It is too inaccessible and remote. It belongs to
another world and cannot quite penetrate this one. Into this gap
between heavenly love and earthly pain, Dickinson pours her own
"broken words." They, and the love they express, are neither high nor
distant nor delayed. They are of this world and are felt within it.
Unlike Christ's "Come unto me all ye that labor and are heavy laden"
(Matthew 11:28), her own language "begins in every place."

Such confrontation between this world and the next is a constant
configuration in Dickinson's writing and is fundamental to her conception of it. Dickinson's characteristic forms reflect her attempt to
refer time to eternity, events to telos—an attempt that is, however,
often threatened with failure. Disruptions in the temporal and tele-

ological orders that are themselves part of a general metaphysical structure have formal consequences; they also determine Dickinson's attitude toward language. Dickinson's work shows a consciousness of language as a subject in its own right. It is not only a medium of expression, but is itself an issue. This extends beyond the familiar tropes of poetic discussions of the poetic act. It involves considerations both of poetry and of language as such. And Dickinson's conception of language, no less than her formal treatments of it, proceeds from her sense that the heavenly and earthly realms no longer stand in proper relation to each other.

This linguistic self-consciousness within a metaphysical framework is not merely accidental. Language held a privileged status in Dickinson's religious tradition. It represented the fundamental mediation between man and God. Through the word, God is known to man, which serves as the primary link between them. Dickinson felt that link to be breaking. This is the impulse behind much of her work. Her own acts of language are generated in response to this breakdown, and her notions of language's role and nature are greatly formed by it. Language becomes essential both in exploring and in attempting to resolve the metaphysical problems she faced. For the problems themselves implicated language. God's word should have been an avenue for reaching him. Instead, it becomes a sign of the difficulty in doing so.

Dickinson's difficulties in interpreting the divine word occur on several levels and reflect her several doubts about its nature. Thus, her reading of creation as God's utterance expresses her questions regarding his role in the world:

> Just as He spoke it from his Hands
> This Edifice remain—
> A Turret more, a Turret less
> Dishonor his Design—
>
> According as his skill prefer
> It perish, or endure—
> Content, soe'er it ornament
> His absent character. [P 848]

The world is a system of signs, issuing from the Godhead. But the poet cannot perceive heavenly love in it. This word declares God's distance rather than his proximity. It demonstrates his refusal to adjust his creation in any way. Accommodation is less to him than the exercise of his own "skill," than the honor of his preordained "Design." Dickinson's invocation of the notion of design has a particular irony. In her context, design was a concept especially tied to involvement in the world. America itself was the product and the special provenance of heavenly design. But Dickinson uses the notion instead to describe God's lack of involvement in the order of events. The created world does not bespeak his interest in, but his indifference to, the needs of his creatures. Thus, the world as word should reveal divinity, but instead conceals it. Creation is an "ornament" to God's "absent character." The sign of him (and "character" may have a particularly lettristic resonance) is one that proclaims him to be not a felt presence but a powerful absence. Or, as she writes in another lettristic image, divine action in creation may only bespeak "A Force illegible" (P 820).

In this poem, God's word takes the form of creation. It also can take the form of Scripture. The Bible is the word of God, who speaks through its events. In Calvin's terms, the biblical text is "that which has proceeded from his mouth and has come to us." As such, it is a fundamental and primary witness to Christ's presence and is the ultimate authority of the church.[1] That the Puritan tradition in America especially elevated scriptural authority, and greatly relied upon typological exegesis of the biblical text, has become the subject of much recent study. Such exegesis first asserts a correspondence and ultimately a concordance between the persons and events of the Old and New Testaments, making the former a figure for the latter. This figuration is in turn extended to the individual soul and, finally, to the ultimate destiny of all things.

In America, this method of reading acquired a central role in the national self-conception. Ursula Brumm proposes the whole notion of covenant theology can be seen as "basically a typological idea."[2] In their daily lives, the Puritans adopted a "remarkable continuous analogy of biblical events," which came to provide "a basis for shaping a powerful cultural vision."[3] The hermeneutic establishes the Bible as prototext for all events in the human life and soul. The self refers itself to biblical patterns; occurrences within and around the self take their place in its eternal design.

For Dickinson, however, as for Melville and Hawthorne, Scripture seems to conceal rather more than it reveals. She questions that the world as word pronounces its Creator. She equally questions that God's written word does so. Biblical reference repeatedly occurs in her work. Many poems are, indeed, exegetical exercises, although almost always for her own contrary purposes:

> "Was not" was all the Statement.
> The Unpretension stuns—
> Perhaps—the Comprehension—
> They wore no Lexicons—
>
> But lest our Speculation
> In inanition die
> Because "God took him" mention—
> That was Philology—   [P 1342]

This is a Dickinsonian commentary on Genesis 5:24: "And Enoch walked with God; and he was not, for God took him." Even more than the mystery of death, the succinctness of its pronouncement—and of its supposed clarification—stuns her. Facing the text, the poet feels the need for further lexical qualification of the stark fact by which a living being becomes nothing. The mere assertion that "God took him" does not explicate the mystery. The "Philology" of biblical language is hardly sufficient for her. Thus, in the guise of commentary that would illuminate the text, she appropriates its words to show how dark and sudden they remain.

Dickinson's uses of exegesis are testaments to her sense of divine incomprehensibility. Both biblical events and the normative purposes of typology are thereby overturned. The Bible becomes a record of divine injustice, instances of which can be repeatedly observed. Abraham's readiness to sacrifice Isaac without a "hesitation" is presented as mere flattery, an "Obeisance" that does not occasion mercy as much as it offsets "Tyranny" (P 1317). Jacob's wrestling with the angel she presents as a victory over the Lord (P 59, L 1042). Elijah's ascension is reduced to "feats inscrutable" (P 1254). And Moses exemplifies all who are not "fairly used" (P 1201). His fate gives particular witness to divine cruelty and caprice:

139

It always felt to me—a wrong
To that Old Moses—done—
To let him see—the Canaan—
Without the entering—

And tho' in soberer moments—
No Moses there can be
I'm satisfied—the Romance
In point of injury—

Surpasses sharper stated—
Of Stephen—or of Paul—
For these—were only put to death—
While God's adroiter will

On Moses—seemed to fasten
With tantalizing Play
As Boy—should deal with lesser Boy—
To prove ability . . .

God's treatment of Moses could be motivated only by his need to prove superior strength. Power, not justice, seems his outstanding attribute, as well as ingenious malice. Moses' punishment is prolonged and is especially painful because incomprehensible. The whole interpretation leads to the suspicion that "No Moses there can be," for doubting the truth of divine action is a short step from doubting the truth of divine record. The biblical words are to be distrusted. Scripture is questioned as a reliable text, and the only lesson the poet draws from it is her own indignation. "Old man on Nebo," the poem concludes, "My justice bleeds—for Thee" (P 597).

Dickinson's inversions of biblical texts, it should be noted, continue to presume a typological method. She seeks, and accepts, biblical models. She finds correlations between herself and its prototypes, even if she prefers rebellious Old Testament figures and binds her defiance to theirs. It cannot, therefore, be claimed without qualification that "it would have been inconsistent for Emily Dickinson to have had a serious interest in typology."[4] Dickinson did have such an interest, not only with regard to particular identifications and correspondences, but, of still greater importance, with regard to the temporal structures entailed in typological conceptions.

Ursula Brumm notes that Saint Paul had conceived of typology "as a model in the temporal sense of its being a pre-figuration of subsequent persons and events." As distinct from symbol, "a reference to the future is essential to it."[5] The relation between terms takes place in the dimension of time and presupposes belief in a unitary, indivisible moment which is God's eternity, to which all discrete, mutable moments are subject, and into which they are ultimately subsumed. "The temporal and causal connection of occurrences is dissolved," writes Erich Auerbach. Each individual occurrence is

> no longer a mere link in an earthly chain of events. It is simultaneously something which has always been and which will be fulfilled in the future; and strictly, in the eyes of God, it is something eternal, something omni-temporal, something already consummated in the realm of fragmentary earthly event.

Typology thus provides an interpretive structure for history, one which, as Auerbach adds, "is magnificent in its homogeneity."[6] In a synecdochic movement, all human time becomes one in God's eternal time, and all history, a reflection of its pattern.

These temporal structures are profoundly implicated in Dickinson's uses of typology. To her, as to Melville in *Moby Dick*, a type is both "a parallel and a prophecy." The events of Scripture situate her own experiences. Through correspondence with the Bible's eternal models, they achieve concordance in the indivisible unity of God's atemporal world. The Bible thus serves to translate and encode the discrete events of experience into eternity's unifying scheme. The importance to her of such atemporal concordance is absolute. She has a precise conception of it. "There is no first, or last, in Forever—It is Centre, there, all the time" (L 288). Of its function, she is no less certain: "This is but a fragment," she laments, "but wholes are not below" (L 656). Figural interpretations, as Auerbach writes, in casting temporal events into a design "at all times present, fulfilled in God's providence, which knows no difference of time,"[7] offers such wholeness and guarantees the fragments below to be truly one with the unity above.

It is with this hope and expectation that Dickinson turns to Scripture, and above all, when she turns to what remains the fullest revelation and the most complete moment known in time. The ultimate figure and antitype is, necessarily, Christ himself. Auerbach emphasizes that it is Christ's sacrament which "gives us the purest picture of the concretely present, the veiled and tentative, the eternal and supratemporal elements contained in the figures."[8] The Incarnation stands at the center of all biblical and historical time. It is the fullness of eternity revealed within a temporal moment, and in it is contained all that is prior and subsequent to it. "His bodily presence," writes Calvin, "was a true and remarkable day of the world, the lustre of which was diffused over all ages. . . . The manifestation of Christ has always darted its rays to a great distance, so as to form one continued day."[9] In this unitary "day," all time is joined. And to its image, Dickinson repeatedly returns. "Gethsemane / —Is but a Province—in the Being's Centre" (P 553), she writes, a state in which many can— and have—partaken:

> Unto like Story—Trouble has enticed me—
> How Kinsmen fell
> Brothers and Sister—who preferred the Glory—
> And their young will
> Bent to the Scaffold, or in Dungeons—chanted—
> Till God's full time—
> When they let go the ignominy—smiling—
> And Shame went still— [P 295]

Martyrdom is an experience whose pattern is eternal. Individual encounters with adversity can find their model not merely as like, but as participating in, such devotional suffering, whose ultimate model is, in the poem, "Crucifixion." Tribulation becomes tropological. Dickinson's own present moment takes place in "God's full time" and is identified with the everlasting moment of the Passion. And this is so for every moment of suffering in history, as the poem's "Brothers and Sister" implies. The date of the poem's composition, 1861, further suggests a historical dimension. The spectacle of "Kinsmen" falling would then be literal.[10] The poem is therefore fully typological, presenting both personal and historical experience as intersecting in the eternity of Christ's sacrifice.

The typological model is, however, not quite fully asserted, either here or in many other Dickinsonian treatments of the Passion. The call toward glory is, in "Unto like Story," named an "Etruscan invitation," something arcane and indecipherable. In other poems, she urges "how others—strove" and "What they—renounced" as a model to herself. But she qualifies the model's acceptance: "Till we are helped— / As if a Kingdom—cared" (P 260). "This World is not Conclusion," she asserts, and she knows that to gain the world to come "Men have borne / Contempt of Generations / And Crucifixion, shown." But the pattern, at best, "beckons" and "baffles," leaving her with a "Faith" that "slips" (P 501).

The Incarnation is not only the focus of all time. It is, as well, the focus of all revelation. The coming of Christ is God's ultimate self-revelation, to which all the rest of Scripture bears witness. The Bible is God's word; but the Son is the very Word of God, the Logos who is himself God, which Scripture serves to attest and make known. Dickinson's hesitation that the biblical narrative truly imparts an eternal pattern finally extends to the Incarnation, not only as event, but as Word. And ultimately, it is in its guise as Logos that God's Word most concerns Dickinson and with the most far-reaching implications. For it is as Logos that God promised to be most accessible to her:

> In the beginning was the Word, and the Word was with God, and the Word was God. The same was in the beginning with God. All things were made by him; and without him was not any thing made that was made. . . . And the Word was made flesh, and dwelt among us, (and we beheld his glory, the glory as the only begotten of the Father,) full of grace and truth. [John 1:1–3,14]

The Gospel according to John proposes that the ultimate form of God's Word is the Logos as Son. "In the theology of the Fourth Gospel, God is unknown and unknowable unless and until he is made known by his Logos, his agent not only in revelation, but also in the creation of the world and the salvation of mankind."[11] Edwin Hatch, in his study of the relation between Greek and Christian ideas, sees John's work as representing a synthesis of Hellenic and Hebraic traditions.

Both the Stoic and the Platonist schools possessed a Logos concept. The Stoics conceived it as the "one law expressing itself in an infinite variety of material forms." The Platonists saw it as the agent by which the eternal Forms "had the power of impressing themselves upon matter."[12] Syncretist tendencies led to a conflation of these different notions, and the Logos emerged as an immutable and eternal principle operating through the manifold world, connecting that world to a world of Forms or Perfection.

An attempt to integrate these Hellenic conceptions with Hebrew thought is already visible in Philo, who relates them to Old Testament notions of the word of God. In the Hebraic tradition, God's word represented communication between divinity and man, as deed and as command. As Rudolph Bultmann writes, unlike the Stoic Logos, "the meaning of which can be understood by itself, and which serves as a principle for comprehending the unity of the cosmic process," the Hebraic word is not "the essence of a system of cosmic laws," but is a "temporal event."[13] It is an act or address that takes place within time and history. Philo, in an effort to interpret Scripture through Greek philosophy, drew a comparison between the word of God and the Greek Logos concept. He tried to combine the Greek cosmological concern—the "concern with explaining the world as it is rather than giving an account of its origin"[14]—with the Hebraic cosmogonical and historical emphasis. In conformity with the latter, Philo accepts the Genesis account of creation. But he also accepts the Hellenic distinction between a world of thought and a world of sense and, therefore, the need for an intermediary between them to act as an agent in fashioning the world. The Logos had already been associated with this function. By loosely identifying the Logos with the creative word of Genesis, Philo achieved a kind of synthesis.

It was John, however, who finally formed this into a doctrine and who fully personified the Logos as the Word of God and the ultimate intermediary between the human and divine worlds. John introduced his conception to a world which, according to E. R. Dodd, widely accepted "the sharp distinction between the eternal or noumenal and the temporal or phenomenal world," as well as "the necessity of mediation between the Supreme Being and the world."[15] The Hellenistic Logos, as part of this conceptual framework, was considered to participate in the noumenal realm and to mediate between it and the phenomenal one. This Logos was exclusively immutable and spiritual, and it was not necessarily personal or personified. John in contrast personifies the Logos and projects it directly into the phenomenal world. "In John the historical life of Jesus is the revelation of God. . . . God is mediated to man in a real person in history, the Logos made flesh."[16] John, in this, injects into the Hellenistic scheme the Hebraic historical element. The metatemporal and metaphenomenal Logos concept becomes a concrete event in time. Revelation becomes focused into a particular person at a particular moment.

Thus, the Logos enters into time and the world. Yet, as Christ's divine nature, it remains immutable and supraphenomenal. John emphasizes its distinction from nature. It is from the beginning, before the creation and with God. If the Hebraic word is "God's action as it works through time," the Johannine Logos, writes Bultmann,

> is not an event recurring within the temporal world, but is eternal Being existent with God from the very beginning. . . . It has a relation to time, but the cosmic and saving event is grounded in the eternity and unity of the divine will; the Logos is not an act of Revelation by God limited to the temporal order, but is pre-existent.[17]

As revelation it is a historical event. But what it reveals is the supramundane, with which it remains identified. And salvation inheres in the avenue to the immutable thus opened. The emphasis remains on the immutable, and the success of mediation depends on a continued ability to accept the immutable in positive relation to the temporal and concrete world. If this relation is shaken, the mediation becomes tenuous, revelation becomes unclear, and the two worlds drift apart.

For Emily Dickinson, this threatens to occur. The supramundane seems increasingly inaccessible; eternity, problematic as an organization of time; and revelation, obfuscated. The Word has receded almost beyond her reach. Its relation to this world has become unstable. Therefore its saving power is uncertain. It can no longer easily serve as conduit from the phenomenal world to the noumenal one. And as Word, this has particular implications for human language:

A Word made Flesh is seldom
And tremblingly partook

Nor then perhaps reported
But have I not mistook
Each one of us has tasted
With ecstasies of stealth
The very food debated
To our specific strength—

A Word that breathes distinctly
Has not the power to die
Cohesive as the Spirit
It may expire if He—
"Made Flesh and dwelt among us"
Could condescension be
Like this consent of Language
This loved Philology.   [P 1651]

This poem, often cited as a statement of Dickinson's aesthetic, opens the problem of the relation between her aesthetic and theology. For the comparison of the process of writing to the Lord's Supper, a recurrent one in Dickinson's verse (compare, for instance, "Your thoughts don't have words every day" [P 1452]) in fact observes the exact structure of the Logos in doctrinal terms and examines in terms consistent with doctrine the possible relations between language and the Logos. In the second stanza, "A Word that breathes distinctly" is compared to the Word made flesh. Like the Logos, it "has not the power to die," it is "Cohesive as the spirit." Both word and Word participate in an immortal and spiritual realm. The Logos, however, is more than a model for language. It is also the ground of language. The word that breathes distinctly is deathless and spiritual, not only like the Logos, but because of it. The relation is dependent. For the poet writes, "It may expire if He—." This thought stops short of completion, but the word *does* is implied. Human language may expire if the Logos does: a possibility almost unspeakable, which the poet interrupts and conceals. The power of human language to communicate with a deathless and spiritual realm only exists if the Logos makes this possible. If "He" expires, human language ceases to be "Cohesive as the spirit."

Such treatment of the Logos as the model and ground of language was most fully explored by Augustine. Augustine compares the divine

Word to the inward word in man's mind and compares the Incarnation to the utterance of an inward word. "And as a word becomes an articulate sound, yet is not changed into one; so the Word of God became flesh, but far be it from us to say He was changed into flesh." He further describes the inward word as dependent on the divine Word for its access to knowledge, truth, and spirit. For Augustine, knowledge is an "incorporeal substance and is the light by which those things are seen that are not seen by carnal eyes." This knowledge is revealed in the Word as Son, which Word is "truly truth . . . and can never have anything false, because it is unchangeable." In becoming flesh, the Word opens immutable truth to man: "And therefore was the Word of God made flesh; in order that we might live rightly through our word following and imitating his example."[18]

Dickinson, too, identifies the Logos with the immutable and spiritual. She too relies on the Incarnation to make that realm accessible: "The import of the Paragraph 'The Word made Flesh,' " she writes; "Had he the faintest intimation Who broached it Yesterday! 'Made Flesh and dwelt among us' " (PF 4). She further considers its relation to an inward word. In the first stanza of her poem, a "Word made flesh," even if "partook," need not be reported. But Dickinson, while invoking the Logos structure, introduces questions as to its adequacy. Besides suggesting that it might expire, she qualifies, in the first stanza, her experience of the Logos as "seldom." Further qualification occurs as it becomes unclear whether she is in fact referring to the Logos at all. "Each one of us has tasted" may refer to either the divine or the phenomenal word; "Ecstasies of stealth" suggests the "food debated" to be personal language, not to be mistaken for the supramundane. The poet leaves open the possibility that phenomenal language is partaken in place of the eternal Word, to its displacement. It is implied that language is distinct from the Logos and is an alternative to it.

Distinction alone need not undermine the structure as a whole. Augustine discusses how the word and the Word are unlike no less than he discusses how they are like. The human Word, having once been "formed" and having come into being, is never equal to the Word "which being neither formless nor formed, itself is eternal and unchangeable substance."[19] But this difference is no barrier to intercourse between them. The one will rely on the other and will pass into eternity through it. They remain complementary. In the work of the Reformers, however, their distinction comes to be emphasized as more radical. Martin Luther insists that

> just as God, the Lord and Creator of all creatures, is immeasurably superior to poor miserable man, who is earth and dust, so there is no analogy between the word of mortal man and the word of the eternal and almighty God. There is a wide gulf between the thoughts, discussions and words of the human heart and those of God.[20]

John Calvin underscores the Johannine choice of the term *flesh* as signifying "the abominable filth" between which and the "spiritual glory of the Speech of God" there is an immeasurably wide distance.[21] Still, for both, this great gulf only makes the miracle of Word become flesh the greater. "There is great emphasis in the contrast of the two words God in flesh," Calvin writes. "How wide the difference between God and man. And yet in Christ we behold the infinite glory of God united to our polluted flesh in such a manner that they became one."[22] The Incarnation does miraculously make it possible to behold the divine glory. It forms a bridge between flesh and spirit, the immeasurably different word and Word.

In Dickinson, this contrast has grown so great that such a bridge is no longer secure. Instead of serving to connect the finite with the infinite, the eternal Logos remains in the eternal world, while human language remains in this one. Distinction becomes nonrelation:

> "Made Flesh and dwelt among us"
> Could condescension be
> Like this consent of Language
> This loved Philology.

This final verse makes clear once more that Dickinson is indeed addressing the theological Logos in this poem, and not only immanent words, if only in order that the former be contrasted with the latter. Language consents to be among us in a way that the Logos does not. The Word no longer condescends to enter into the human world. That which has been indirectly hinted throughout the poem is finally declared. The seldom experienced Word made flesh competes with the word tasted with "ecstasies of stealth." It has possibly expired as ground or justification for the human word. It is no longer in this world. Instead, there is only "this loved Philology."

The general possibility of modeling language on the Logos is discussed by Kenneth Burke in *The Rhetoric of Religion*. There Burke develops a construction that is essentially Augustinian. Burke draws analogies between how words function and theological structures. As in Augustine, the Father is to the Son "as the thought that leads to utterance is to the uttered word that expresses the thought." Burke similarly draws a parallel between words and spirit: "Words are to the non-verbal things they name as Spirit is to Matter. That is, if we equate the non-verbal with 'nature,' . . . then verbal or symbolic action is analogous to the 'grace' that is said to 'perfect' nature." For Burke, the analogy remains figurative. For Dickinson, however, verbal action and the meanings it articulates do in fact derive from the world of spirit. A disruption in her relation to that world would have verbal consequences, as well as consequences for meaning. "The realm of the symbolic corresponds (in our analogy) to the realm of the supernatural," writes Burke.[23] It is exactly this analogy that Dickinson is questioning. In her treatment of the Logos structure, she does not merely duplicate it, as Burke does, nor does she accept it as figurative. For her, the relation between words and spirit must be actual. She therefore reconsiders the model as a whole in an effort to resolve the problems it raises for her. Through language, she expresses and explores her doubts concerning the relations between heaven and earth, and, through language, she attempts to redeem the religious structures which have become uncertain. It becomes, in this, both medium and instrument. Her theological conflicts have linguistic ramifications, and language has for her a theological importance. As a primary tie between heaven and earth, their disrupted relation effects both her use and her conception of language. And language becomes an image and a means for Dickinson's efforts to restore the relations that have become disrupted.

Dickinson at times positively asserts the structure in which language, as God's Word, does redeem. Through the Word man then has access to heaven, as a spiritual being communing with the world of spirit:

I heard, as if I had no Ear
Until a Vital Word
Came all the way from Life to me
And then I knew I heard.

I saw, as if my Eye were on
Another, till a Thing
And now I know 'twas Light, because
It fitted them, came in.

I dwelt, as if Myself were out,
My Body but within
Until a Might detected me
And set my kernel in.

And Spirit turned into the Dust
"Old Friend, thou knowest me,"
And Time went out to tell the News
And met Eternity.   [P 1039]

"In him was life, and the life was the light of men" (John 1:4): the
Johannine Gospel resounds through the "Vital Word" of this poem,
which comes from "Life" and is "Light." It raises the "Ear" and "Eye"
from the sensible level which perceives "Another" to the spiritual
level which truly hears and sees. And just as in the fourth Gospel the
Logos bestows the "power to become the sons of God," so the "Vital
Word" is a "Might" which empowers the inward self, raising it from
body to the true "kernel" of spirit. Through this, the spirit knows that
it is distinct from dust. Through this, the soul is released from time
into eternity.

In this poem, a distinction between heaven and earth, spirit and
flesh, is assumed. But the two do not conflict. The Logos provides a
bridge for crossing from the former to the latter. In other poems,
however, the distinction becomes an obstacle which the Logos cannot
overcome. Itself partaking in the divine, it partakes in the difficulties
that Dickinson feels arise in aligning the divine and the human:

Not in this World to see his face—
Sounds long—until I read the place
Where this—is said to be
But just the Primer—to a life—

Unopened—rare—Upon the Shelf—
Clasped yet—to Him—and me—

And yet—My Primer suits me so
I would not choose—a Book to know
Than that—be sweeter wise—
Might some one else—so learned—be
And leave me—just my A—B—C—
Himself—could have the Skies— [P 418]

Language in this poem is in at least one aspect the language of Scripture, which seems here to refer to a Pauline rather than a Johannine text: "For now we see through a glass, darkly; but then face to face" (I Cor. 13:12). According to Paul, this world is but the prologue to a world to come; and his text may be that "Primer to a life" in which the poet at the outset reads. That primer may be, as well, a figure for this life represented as a text in its own right, as is the life to come—which, however, is as yet "Unopened." Finally, the face to be seen is also a word: for the Logos is the manifestation of the Father, the Father made visible: "No one can know the Father except by the Word of God, that is by the Son revealing Him . . . for all things are manifested by the Word."[24] In this Word, the other words conjoin. For the Word as Son subsumes Scripture; the Logos is God's agent in revelation as in creation. And through the Logos the life to come, although still "Upon the Shelf," is "Clasped yet—to Him—and me." Holding the Logos, the poet holds to the world where she will see face to face.

For these various words to remain coherent among their interreferences, the poet must retain her sense that they all participate in one another. God's word, as Scripture and as Logos, although constituting an otherworldly text, must also be legible in this world. The Son as Word must be within reach if his truth is to be manifested here. But the poem strongly associates the Logos with the world to come, seen "Not in this world," and in the second stanza, it projects a consequent dissociation between the texts of this world and that of the next. The poet asserts that the life she has suffices her, not as a preface, but as complete in itself: "My Primer suits me so / I would not choose a Book to know / Than that." If there be any who think some other text "sweeter wise," he is welcome to the skies. God's

Word, as an otherworldly text, is dismissed. The poet chooses over it "just my A—B—C," the letters of this world, without reference to any further text.

No Word participates both in this world and in the next. They remain separate realms with the Logos relegated to the latter. And the poet seems to be left only with language as such. She therefore could attempt to dispense with God's Word altogether and to embrace in its stead an entirely immanent language. Human language would assume the role previously held by language of and as the transcendent world. Dickinson's poetry traces her gestures in this direction, in which language is granted powers of the divine Word:

> He ate and drank the precious Words—
> His Spirit grew robust—
> He knew no more that he was poor,
> Nor that his frame was Dust—
>
> He danced along the dingy Days
> And this Bequest of Wings
> Was but a Book—What Liberty
> A loosened spirit brings—   [P 1587]

Words are announced and their power is asserted. They strengthen and release man from his poverty and dust. He is liberated from the "dingy Days" of mortality which thus cease to define him. But in this poem, it is no longer necessary that it is indeed the Logos that bestows these gifts. This "Bequest of Wings" the poet ascribes to "but a Book," which could be Scripture or the Logos; but it could be any book as well. The same ambiguity is felt when Dickinson writes in another poem that poetry and love are "coeval" and that to experience them is to be consumed: "For None see God and live" (P 1247). It is unclear whether poetry is an ultimate image of God or whether God has become a metaphor for poetry, which acquires his attributes. Divine functions are suggested as devolving onto human language.

Dickinson at times seems to delight in sustaining such ambiguities—which pose, however, mutually exclusive alternatives. In another poem devoted to poetics, the exact role of the secular and the sacred word is stated through a masterful syntactic obfuscation:

Shall I take thee, the Poet said,
To the propounded word?
Be stationed with the Candidates
Till I have finer tried—

The Poet searched Philology
And when about to ring
For the suspended Candidate
There came unsummoned in—

That portion of the Vision
The Word applied to fill
Not unto nomination
The Cherubim reveal—   [P 1126]

Dickinson presents poetic word selection as inspired drama. What is
unclear, however, is the source of inspiration. At first, only the mundane words of philology seem at issue. But then comes unsummoned
a vision that may be transcendent or immanent. Certainly it seems
noumenal. But whether it actually originates in a higher world and is
bestowed on the poet as a sacred gift, or whether it is sacred as the gift
of the poet herself, is left for the two final lines. And these sustain
antithetical readings. Either Dickinson is asserting that the ultimate
vision is not subject to human nomination but rather is revealed by
Cherubim, or she is declaring her vision as not subject to the nomination which Cherubim reveal. Either reading seems possible; their
divergent implications cannot be reconciled.

In other poems, ambiguity becomes boldness. Dickinson openly
asserts that music ascends to "something upper wooing us / But not
to our Creator" (P 1480). She turns to poetry for consolation: "Martyr
Poets . . . seek in Art—the Art of Peace" (P 544). The poet is "Exteri-
or—to Time" (P 448). The "Name" of "One who could repeat the
Summer day" remains when all else has passed away (P 307). As God
recedes from Dickinson's grasp, language comes forward as a possible alternative:

I reckon—when I count at all—
First—Poets—Then the Sun—
Then Summer—Then the Heaven of God—
And then—the List is done—

But, looking back—the First so seems
To Comprehend the Whole—
The Others look a needless Show—
So I write—Poets—All—

Their Summer—lasts a Solid Year—
They can afford a Sun
The East—would deem extravagant—
And if the Further Heaven—

Be Beautiful as they prepare
For those who worship Them—
It is too difficult a Grace—
To justify the Dream—   [P 569]

Poets are the consummate beings. They provide the ultimate stance for "looking back" from which all is put into perspective. They "Comprehend the Whole." They conquer time, granting Dickinson that eternity for which she so longs. In all, they accrue the all-encompassing, metatemporal, absolute nature of gods. Their art is paradise, and they are to be worshipped. The poem approaches an aestheticism in which religion is replaced by art.

The last stanza, however, reveals this elevation of art to be relative rather than absolute. Underlying the apotheosis of poets is an opprobrium of the divine Creator. Art constitutes a paradise because the "Further Heaven" has proved "too difficult a Grace—To justify the Dream." The apparent displacement of the Creator by creators is revealed as a statement, not about poets, but about God. It proceeds from a sense that heaven, with its difficult demands and its difficult distance, can no longer be justified.

This poem is not aestheticist, it is critique. The interest in language for its own sake is a function of lost proximity to the divine. Language is thus not finally defined in relation to itself as a closed, self-contained system. "Further Heaven" remains as the second term against which language continues to be measured. The poet may assert a preference for the language she possesses, but she does so in contradistinction to the world which she feels has escaped her grasp.

Emily Dickinson's poetry has often been interpreted in aestheticist terms. It is argued that poetry came to serve a religious function for her or that religion became a fiction for her poetry. According to Charles Anderson, consciousness, and more particularly the artist's consciousness, becomes the realm of truth. Poets "can create both heaven and earth, a heaven more attainable, and a nature more satisfying than any the real world can offer."[25] Robert Weisbuch similarly writes that "death and its aftermath is . . . raw material for speculations, and even for speculations about the limits of speculation"; "poetry is the mind's continual thrust toward the ungraspable, as questing rather than completed vision, could replace the goal of heaven."[26] Sharon Cameron, in *Lyric Time*, consistently projects her own conceptions of fiction onto Dickinson. According to Cameron, immortality is for Dickinson a poetic construction, and poetry is not only its image but its locus. Language provides "occasions of presence" that

> gain the self the only immortality it will ever know, for in a very real sense they lie outside of time. . . . presence is not yet weakened by the realization that immortality is an illusion. In its dissociation from action, its repudiation of necessity, lies strength, a redemptive counter to the dutiful complicity that characterizes our lives.[27]

But Emily Dickinson ultimately rejects poetry and language as a religious sphere in the church's stead. Instead of embracing language as an independent and self-sustaining power, she considers it in these terms and denies its efficacy. In a poem exalting the ecstasy that poetry inspires and that inspires poetry, Dickinson asserts the power of language only to trace that power's collapse:

> It would never be Common—more—I said—
> Difference—had begun—
> Many a bitterness—had been—
> But that old sort—was done—
>
> Or—if it sometime—showed—as 'twill—
> Upon the Downiest—Morn—
> Such bliss—had I—for all the years—
> 'Twould give an Easier—pain—
>
> I'd so much joy—I told it—Red—
> Upon my simple Cheek—

> I felt it publish—in my Eye—
> 'Twas needless—any speak—
>
> I walked—as wings—my body bore—
> The feet—I former used—
> Unnecessary—now to me—
> As boots—would be—to Birds—
>
> I put my pleasure all abroad—
> I dealt a word of Gold
> To every Creature—that I met—
> And Dowered—all the World—

A transformation has occurred; the longed-for release has come. Old bitterness is left behind, and a different, uncommon condition is announced. The third and fourth stanzas begin to define this new condition. "Told" and "publish" hint that the joy expressed through blush and eye is poetic. No one else need speak, for the poet will do so. The image of bird flight reinforces this as an aesthetic transformation. Like Shelley's skylark, Keats's nightingale, and other romantic birds, the poet here too sprouts wings and soars above the earth in poetic flight.

The following stanza makes the identification between the announced euphoria and poetic transport explicit. Language constitutes exuberance, joy, and wealth, not only for the poet, but through the poet, for the world. Her "word of Gold" is distributed freely, a gift to every creature who, thus endowed, partakes of the poet's power. Not only the poet, but the world is transformed through the creative act.

Still, there is a note of warning. The second stanza offers a *concessio*. The change is not absolute. Bitterness still shows itself of a morning. Conceding this seems, nevertheless, ground only for a stronger affirmation. The present bliss, the poet seems to say, compensates all former difficulties as well as those that remain. This affirmation of bliss, however, is set in the conditional tense: "'Twould give an easier pain." The syntactic hesitation is concealed at the outset, and the poem's first stanzas seem unqualified praise of poetic power. It is left to the remaining stanzas to define and dramatize the warning:

> When—suddenly—my Riches shrank—
> A Goblin—drank my Dew—

My Palaces—dropped tenantless—
Myself—was beggared—too—

I clutched at sounds—
I groped at shapes—
I touched the tops of Films—
I felt the Wilderness roll back
Along my Golden lines—

The Sackcloth—hangs upon the nail—
The Frock I used to wear—
But where my moment of Brocade—
My—drop—of India?   [P 430]

The poet's riches have vanished without warning. She can no longer dower the world, but is herself left beggared. All that had transpired is undone. The invigorating dew evaporates, the linguistic palaces crumble. Language itself disintegrates in dispersed sounds and dissolved shapes. Before, the words had distributed gold, making the world glisten in its own image. Now the golden lines "roll back," undoing what they had wrought, disarranging the linguistic structures that had before seemed the arranging force. The poetic Eden reverts to wilderness. And the poet returns to the condition that was hers before the poetic transport came to her. Art is revealed, not as a transforming power, but as a costume. Imagination's brocade fades into sackcloth. The drop of India—as exotica and as ink—vanishes. Aesthetic ecstasy proves a passing moment and not a true rebirth.

This poem perhaps merely describes the passing of poetic inspiration. But in recognizing that such inspiration passes, the poem recognizes the distinction between linguistic power and a power that does not pass away. The gold of language perishes. It cannot be maintained as the source enriching the world and translating wilderness into palace. Language collapses as an independent principle. It is not omnipotent, but limited. It cannot by itself bring chaos to order. Language, instead, reverts back into chaos.

Dickinson does at times insist on the self-sufficiency of her art. But she finally could neither discard heaven as a fiction nor replace it with fictions of her own making. Attempts to turn to art eventually demonstrate its inability to fulfill such a ministry. With her Auditor "Passive as Granite," she feels that "Sobbing—will suit—as well as psalm" (P 261). Having endured a "Night," she finds that her soul's "Strings were snapt / Her Bow to Atoms blown." Its song is unable to rescue her from "Madness" (P 410). What remains to her is a sense of disjunction between her own language and the source that would sustain it:

Warm in her Hand these accents lie
While faithful and afar
The Grace so awkward for her sake
Its fond subjection wear—   [P 1313]

Praise of the warmth and proximity of "these accents" as opposed to grace proceeds because, however "awkward for her sake" grace might be, it remains "afar" compared to her own words. The ascendance of the latter is a measure of the default of the former. The poem raises language above Logos, but Logos remains as subject, undercutting the independence of language as itself a saving power. Dickinson does not finally resolve the dissociation between her words and the power that truly saves by establishing language as a separate sphere. The disjunction of earth from heaven, of language from the Word, constitutes for Dickinson the problem, not the solution.

But if poetry does not itself constitute a realm that redeems experience from disorder, it does afford Dickinson her best hope of re-establishing a link to the realm that can. She could not accept Heaven when conceived as too distant from mutability to be its ordering principle. But in and through language, Dickinson strives to construct a model for a relation to the infinite both possible and positive. Language becomes for her an arc bridging the other world and this one, not by displacing this world for the next, but by drawing eternity into temporal reality. Language then represents the order of paradise as penetrating this world's disorder, the power of infinity as endowing the finite world:

For this—accepted Breath—
Through it—compete with Death—
The fellow cannot touch this Crown—
By it—my title take—
Ah, what a royal sake
To my necessity—stooped down!

No Wilderness—can be
Where this attendeth me—
No Desert Noon
No fear of frost to come
Haunt the perennial bloom—
But Certain June!

Get Gabriel—to tell—the royal syllable—
Get Saints—with new—unsteady tongue—
To say what trance below
Most like their glory show—
Fittest the Crown!   [P 195]

Language seems at first to have displaced the divine Word. Through her own "Breath," the poet can withstand mortality. From it she takes her title. The "Breath," however, is presented as an offering. It is "accepted," and its power is shown to derive from the "royal sake" that has condescended to the poet's necessity, as Christ condescended to bear flesh. This is human language invested with a power whose source remains divine. It is equally a divine language that has descended into the human word, opening to man a world above which is also figured as linguistic. Elsewhere Dickinson describes the entrance into heaven as an awakening to the "Archangel's syllables" (P 194), as an ear greeting "the sounds of Welcome—there" (P 431). Here, too, Gabriel's "royal syllable" is the power that has responded to her need, as it did in descending from heaven to explain Daniel's prophetic vision.[28] Gabriel shall "tell" how the trance below can most reflect the divine glory. She names his word as the link between above and below and asks that it enter the world so that human language can best articulate in its own terms the mystery of transcendence.

With Gabriel's response, the heavenly Word could inform earthly discourse. In this poem, Gabriel's is not an eternal, transcendent utterance demanding that man be raised to heaven to hear or to understand it. It is announced with a "new—unsteady tongue" that does not so much pronounce as unfold into human language attesting and iterating it. The "Crown" of election is attained through a breath accepted above and spoken below. There, it attends the poet, as fluent rather than static, as immanent rather than exclusively transcendent. The Word moves with the word in a process which is this-worldly, but is directed, and therefore ordered, by a higher power.

This investment of the word with the Word represents Dickinson's most concerted effort at resolving the problem of disjunction she experienced between the two worlds. It is, however, an effort that remains plagued by inconsistencies never fully resolved. Dickinson remains caught in the dichotomy she tries to overcome. At times she envisions a music whose place "is in the Human Heart / And in the Heavenly Grace" (P 1585); but her conception of heaven and the Word as fixed in an eternity that cannot be reconciled to time persists. She continues to see it as an alternative which, if chosen, must displace the mortal world. For the "Gift" of afterlife, she feels, "we gave the Earth / And mortgaged Heaven" (P 1706). She can either embrace this life and lose the life to come, or gain the life to come and lose this life.

This conflict inevitably raises the question of Dickinson's own withdrawal from the world. Reclusion as a religious act represents an extreme consequence of a structure in which devotion to God entails denial of this world. That Dickinson viewed her own seclusion as a form of devotion is evident when she refers to herself as a bride of Christ, a nun, or a martyr.[29] In this she followed a precedent urged, for example, in the anchorite text *The Wohunge of Ure Lauerd:*

> A Wrecche bodi and a wac bere ich over eorthe, and that swuche as hit is have yiven and yive wile to thi servise, mi bodi henge with thi bodi neiled o rode, sperred querfaste withinne fowr wahes, and henge I wile with the and neaver mare of mi rode cume til that I deie.[30]

To be oneself crucified within four walls is here the highest form of *imitatio Christi*, an imitation fully expounded by Thomas a Kempis, whose work Dickinson avidly read.[31]

Dickinson did not fail to see this aspect of her withdrawal. But her attitude was determined as much by defiance as by devotion. It is with a strange wit that she wrote, after many years indoors, that her neighbors knew her "by faith" (L 727), or that while God is conceived as omnipresent, "yet we always think of Him as somewhat of a recluse" (L 551). It is an odd *imitatio* that cites heaven's shyness of earth as its exemplar: "Bashful Heaven—thy Lovers small / Hide— too—from thee" (P 703). Dickinson's renunciation was an act of ambivalence, as much defense as quest. In 1858, she wrote to Samuel Bowles: "I am sorry you came, because you went away. Hereafter, I will pick no rose, lest it fade or prick me" (L 189). Soon after, she wrote to Mrs. Joseph Haven, "I am glad I did not know you better, since it would have grieved me more that you went away" (L 192). Having and hoping perilously threaten through the potential lack and despair they make possible. Poem after poem in Dickinson's opus warns that "For each ecstatic instant / We must an anguish pay" (P 125). Unlike those Henry James characters who choose to renounce after having undergone experience, Dickinson renounced before experience could injure her. To defend against inevitable loss, she would possess nothing. It is better not to have than to have and lose: "When one has given up One's life / The parting with the rest / Feels easy" (P 853).

Renunciation thus had a dual aspect. And even if Dickinson withdrew as an act of religious devotion, she did so to protect herself from a world of time and change which she found unendurable and which could not but implicate its Creator. Her withdrawal hence remains a form of religious challenge, either in hatred of a God she could not entirely deny or in paradoxical service to Him she doubted. It was, in either case, an extreme and contradictory measure. Even her poem most cited as defending renunciation seems rather to incarnate her contrary notions regarding it: at best it is a "piercing Virtue," a "putting out of Eyes" (P 745), the violence of which is unmistakable, and which argues, as Sharon Cameron explains, Dickinson's attempt "to convince herself of something she finds both difficult and imperative to believe—that renunciation is a virtue; that it is piercing, she knows."[32] That such violence is requisite most indicts a structure in which the world and God are so at odds that the choice of one precludes involvement with the other. The act of renunciation enacts above all a sense that time and eternity remain irreconcilable and mutually exclusive, a sense that Dickinson could never quite conquer. She must value eternal wholeness for mutability to be coherent. But eternity seemed unrelenting in its demand that for its sake the mutable be renounced. Dickinson thus remained caught between the worlds:

Without this—there is nought—
All other Riches be
As is the Twitter of a Bird—
Heard opposite the Sea—

I could not care—to gain
A lesser than the Whole—
For did not this include themself—
As Seams—include the Ball?

I wished a way might be
My Heart to subdivide—
'Twould magnify—the Gratitude—
And not reduce—the Gold—   [P 655]

The poet finds anything less than the synecdochic and absolute "Whole" insufficient. Without it, nothing has value. But that whole should not be external to or distinct from the "Seams" which constitute it and which it contains. The discrete and the complete should interpenetrate and be continuous one with the other. And yet, the poet admits that this is not the case. She wishes that "Gratitude" to the whole would not exclude the "Gold" of present partial experience. But she cannot successfully balance her allegiance. The claims of one seem to exclude rather than include the claims of the other. She must choose either all the "Other Riches" she has or the one endowment she cannot do without, but which is gained only at absolute cost.

The ultimate ramifications of this irreconcilable positing of time and eternity against each other are, for Dickinson as poet, its consequences in the world of discourse. Torn between the two, Dickinson is finally torn with regard to the speech act itself. The world of language is the world of time and change, which an exclusive devotion to the immutable would preclude, but which a complete exclusion of the immutable would render impossible. If there is no mediator or continuity between them, they come to seem radical alternatives. But to truly choose either would equally defeat discourse. The immutable world would subsume mutable language; mutable language, without transcendent sanction, would collapse. Choosing either the one or the other would make utterance impossible. It would entail the choice of silence.

A tension between silence and speech is consequently felt throughout Dickinson's work. Each involves both positive and negative elements. In "I felt a Cleaving in my Mind," silence represents a failure to articulate, derived in the failure of order and coherence:

I felt a Cleaving in my Mind
As if my Brain had split—
I tried to match it—Seam by Seam—
But could not make them fit.

The thought behind, I strove to join
Unto the thought before—
But Sequence ravelled out of Sound
Like Balls—upon a Floor.   [P 937]

Totality and division act here as the two poles determining co-herence and its lack. In a failure of synecdoche, parts will neither stand for nor take their place in wholes. The "Ball" of complete containment unravels as the poet's unity of thought breaks apart. And with the collapse of unity comes that of sequence; with the collapse of sequence comes that of sound. Only an orderly unfolding can sustain articulate discourse. Dickinson continues to conceive such orderly unfolding as grounded in a unitary totality. When wholeness fails, articulation fails. Silence is a result of dispersion.

Silence can contribute to, as well as proceed from, such disorder. In her letters, Dickinson presents language as a stay against confusion: "I felt a palsy here—the verses just relieve," she wrote to Higginson (L 265). Confusion can, however, overpower: "To speak seemed taken from me—Blow has followed blow, till the wondering terror of the Mind clutches what is left, helpless of an accent" (L 792). Conversely, silence can be a contributing cause to the fall of reason. Thus in one poem she describes "A not admitting of the wound / Until it grew so wide / That all my Life had entered it" [P 1123]. Silence, here, is boundless and infinite. But it is so as a sign of dissolution. The failure of expression reflects a failure of apprehension and of internal cohe-sion. Expression may even have mitigated the impact of experience by placing it into a linguistic order. That it has not done so augments the confusion and reinforces the status of silence as a realm of disorder.

Silence as linguistic and ontological failure is similarly enjoined against heaven. It serves as an accusation against, and an image of divine distance. "I have a King, who does not speak," Dickinson writes (P 103). "I know that He exists / Somewhere— in Silence" (P 338). To Judge Lord, she wrote, "Prayer has not an answer, and yet how many pray" (L 790). Death joins this constellation of imagery. It too is a silent world, which "Once to achieve, annuls the power / Once to communicate" (P 922). "Immortality" is that which does not "Confirm—by Word" (P 679). As she summarizes, "The Living tell— / The Dying—but a Syllable— / The Coy Dead—None" (P 408).

Silence thus becomes a Dickinsonian figure for the inaccessibility of the other world and the disorder to which this gives rise. It also represents, however, her acceptance of the other world as the realm of truth and spirit. "The Tomb / who tells no secret" she calls "True" (P 408). She praises the "Noon" of immortality as "Phraseless" (P 297). Death makes "no syllable" because it is a "Sublimer sort—than Speech" (P 310). Silence is the highest expression of the deepest emotion. "Best Grief" is "Tongueless" (P 793). Gratitude is a "still appreciation" (P 989). "Exhilaration" transports us where "statement is not found" (P 1118). And silence is the truest language of the soul. The "Growth of man" must "achieve—Itself / Through the solitary prowess / Of a Silent Life" (P 750). At the white heat, the soul burns as a "finer Forge That soundless tugs—within" (P 365).

The inward word of the soul is raised above vocal utterance. Spoken language takes place in the material world. Its "Sound" is relegated to the "smaller Ear / Outside" (P 733), while the unspoken word is a "foliage of the mind . . . Of no corporeal kind" (P 1634). It, unlike the spoken word, represents and participates in the immutable and incorporeal world of spirit, to which Dickinson explicitly refers it:

> Speech is one symptom of Affection
> And Silence one—
> The perfectest communication
> Is heard of none—
>
> Exists and its indorsement
> Is had within—
> Behold, said the Apostle,
> Yet had not seen! [P 1681]

Peter had described the "joy unspeakable" of a faith in Christ "Whom having not seen, ye love" (I Peter 1:8). Dickinson here parallels faith in things invisible and spiritual to words inaudible and "within." Unspoken affection is a higher expression than spoken affection. The silence of the word in the soul is the "perfectest communication."

In elevating the inward word, Dickinson's position approaches Augustine's. For him, "the word that sounds outwardly is the sign of the word that gives light inwardly." The inward word is in turn closest to the spiritual realm:

> We conceive and beget the word within from the things we have beheld in the eternal truth . . . and we have the true knowledge of things, thence conceived, as it were a word within us, and by speaking we beget it from within.

Finally, the inward word is most like, as well as closest to, the divine Word: "The likeness of the Divine Word is to be sought not in our outer and sensible word but in the inner and mental one."[33] Dickinson, too, makes these comparisons. For her, the immutable "Day at Summer's Full" is one when:

> The time was scarce profaned, by speech—
> The symbol of a word
> Was needless, as at Sacrament,
> The Wardrobe—of our Lord—   [P 322]

Just as flesh is mere expression of the Logos, so the word is mere symbol to the poet's experience of fullness. It is, as such, not only superfluous, but profaning. A pure sense of the other world, and communion with it, is obtained through muteness. The sacrament that joins the self to heaven is, when least adulterated, unencumbered by sound.

In adopting what can be called an Augustinian model of signification, Dickinson implicitly accepts a word structure that separates, in the language of sign theory, the signified meaning from the outward expression which acts only as its signifier. And the first, signified term is identified, as Jacques Derrida has shown, with a transcendent, immutable realm:

> Linguistic science cannot therefore hold on to the difference between signifier and signified—the very idea of the sign—without the difference between the sensible and intelligible, certainly, but also not without retaining more profoundly and more implicitly and by the same token the reference to a signified able to "take place" in its intelligibility, before its "fall," before any expulsion into the exteriority of the sensible

here below. As the face of pure intelligibility, it refers to an absolute logos to which it is immediately united. This absolute logos was an infinite creative subjectivity in medieval theology; the intelligible face of the sign remains turned toward the word and the face of God.[34]

The signifier remains external to the true meaning of thought and finally is intrusive with regard to it. Dickinson, just so, identifies the signified thought with fullness and inwardness, and the signifying "symbol of the word" with the external and incomplete. The latter can never equal the former. At best it can duplicate, at worst profane, the signified truth it embodies.

Dickinson's attitude toward articulated language is consequently mixed:

> To tell the Beauty would decrease
> To state the Spell demean—
> There is a syllable-less Sea
> Of which it is the sign—
> My will endeavors for its word
> And fails, but entertains
> A Rapture as of Legacies—
> Of introspective Mines—   [P 1700]

True beauty is beyond speech. It is the "sign" of a "syllable-less Sea," a silent word reflecting a spiritual silence. To tell it would demean it. Thus, in failing to find words for her thought, the poet only affirms her rapture. As in Augustine, the outward word signifies an inward experience. And the inward experience is in greater proximity with, and partakes in, the world of silent truth, the "Estate perpetual," as Dickinson elsewhere names it (P 855).

For Augustine, however, external language reflects internal, and internal reflects the divine. The word within reaches to the divine through the Word. There is a series of gradations through which the visible and audible enters into the invisible and inaudible. Augustine's own words take their place in this series, and both move and guide from the former to the latter. For Dickinson, the links in this series have grown tenuous. The two worlds, without mediation or continuity, come into opposition. As the "syllable-less Sea" seems more distant, as mediation between it and corporeal shores seems less possible, silence and speech too become opposed. Language then comes to seem either a betrayal of the inward spiritual word or mere gibberish without it. This is Dickinson's condition; she seems faced at best with a choice between them, which she, however, cannot make.

Identifying truth with silence has obvious implications for the act of publishing. Dickinson's steadfast refusal to publish, even in spite of strong pressure from Helen Hunt Jackson, in many ways reenacts the ambivalence of her reclusion and the multivalence of her silences.[35] Surely it reflects her abhorrence of exposure to the world of unpredictable change. But her public silence also follows from her sense that speech betrays the immortal world which remained its ground. It is in these terms that she explains her stance in a famous poem:

Publication—is the Auction
Of the Mind of Man—
Poverty—be justifying
For so foul a thing

Possibly—but We—would rather
From Our Garret go
White—Unto the White Creator—
Than invest—Our Snow—

Thought belong to Him who gave it—
Then—to Him Who bear
Its Corporeal illustration—Sell
The Royal Air—

In the Parcel—Be the Merchant
Of the Heavenly Grace—
But reduce no Human Spirit
To Disgrace of Price—   [P 709]

The language of contract, familiar to Dickinson's relation with God, asserts here that thought and its expression are committed to heaven.[36] Publication would betray the compact and debase what is in its essence an inward communion. Rather than "invest" the snowlike purity of private utterance, the poet would go "White unto the White Creator." For "Thought" is bestowed by the supramundane and retains its ties to it; therefore it must be devoted to the world of spirit.

Intercourse with the mundane world, outward expression, would be the sin of simony. It would disgrace and even befoul the spiritual world by bringing it into too close contact with the material one.

This notion of discourse as fallen comes to assume a Pauline cast. Paul urges the distinction between the "natural body" sown in corruption and the "spiritual body" raised in glory (I Cor. 15:42–43). He preaches that "flesh and blood cannot inherit the kingdom of God; neither doth corruption inherit incorruption" (I Cor. 15:50). And he identifies the incorruptible spirit with the inward word, the corrupt flesh with the outward one: "Forasmuch as ye are manifestly declared to be the epistle of Christ ministered by us, written not with ink, but with the Spirit of the living God" (II Cor. 3:3). Dickinson likewise assumes that what is outwardly published is in subjection to a "Corporeal Illustration," whereas devotional silence fulfills its commitment to "Heavenly Grace" and preserves the value of the "Human Spirit." Within this configuration, heaven, spirit, and silence supercede and abrogate earth, matter, and articulation. Devotion to eternity seems to preclude intercourse with the mutable world and, therefore, utterance in the mutable, material medium of its language.

But Dickinson is hard pressed to accept fully this configuration. Herself pronouncing the words of Paul's mockers in II Corinthians, she insists, "And with what Body do they come?" (L 671). She writes of Heaven, "I hope it is not so unlike earth that we shall miss the particular form" (L 671). The world of forms, of matter, and of palpable signs is the only one she could conceive; she is loathe to let it go. "Without any body," she writes after her father's death and asks, "What kind can that be?" (L 471). The incorporeal realm beyond body and beyond sign is not apprehensible and forgoes too much. Each aspect—spiritual and corporeal—seems necessary rather than inimical to the other. And certainly, each remains necessary to language:

> The Spirit lasts—but in what mode—
> Below, the Body speaks,
> But as the Spirit furnishes—
> Apart, it never talks—
> The Music in the Violin
> Does not emerge alone

But Arm in Arm with Touch, yet Touch
Alone—is not a Tune—
The Spirit lurks within the Flesh
Like Tides within the Sea
That make the Water live, estranged
What would the Either be?   [P 1576]

Integration and reconciliation between the two aspects alone could resolve the separate claims made by a spirit which in itself "never talks" and a body which speaks "as the Spirit furnishes." Both are necessary to nature and to utterance: to the sea that lives only through the motion of its tide; to the music whose tune is a function of touch. One aspect estranged from the other would obviate both, whereas mutual consecration of each by each would permit both to be affirmed.

This seems to the poet salutary and necessary, and she seeks to express this interfusion. But, like Emerson, who also attempted to assert an "instant dependence of form upon soul," an "essential dependence of the material world on thought and volition," Dickinson is finally unable to do so. Emerson's teaching of the "incarnation of the spirit in a form—in forms, like my own" strives toward a nondualistic notion of expression. The "form" and its "thought" act together indivisibly. But Emerson's efforts finally collapse into the dualism implied by the very terms of spirit and form. He is carried by the impetus of this terminology to explain that "one of the facts we contemplate is external and fugitive; and the other is permanent and connate with the soul."[37] The split between the two spheres reemerges. The permanent stands against the fugitive, the soul, against the external world of matter. Dickinson, too, finally remains within this conceptual world, which is essentially dualistic, and she continues to feel the conflicting claims of each of its terms.

This opposition Dickinson never overcomes. But she, while remaining within its confines, continues to protest the exclusion of one term by the other. She mocks the attempt to distinguish some invisible, otherworldly "Music" from actual, palpable "Sound" (P 501). Above all, she protests the necessity of choosing between them. The rebellion against what seemed the inescapable unjustness of heavenly demands she applies finally to language, which, following the system's logic she feels called upon to renounce, but which she resists renouncing:

> The single Screw of Flesh
> Is all that pins the Soul
> That stands for Deity, to Mine
> Upon my side the Veil—
>
> Once witnessed of the Gauze—
> Its name is put away
> As far from mine, as if no plight
> Had printed yesterday,
>
> In tender—solemn Alphabet,
> My eyes just turned to see,
> When it was smuggled by my sight
> Into Eternity—
>
> More Hands—to hold—These are but Two—
> One more new—mailed Nerve
> Just granted, for the Peril's sake—
> Some striding—Giant—Love—
>
> So greater than the Gods can show,
> They slink before the Clay,
> That not for all their Heaven can boast
> Will let its Keepsake—go   [P 263]

Here are aligned the various terms of Dickinson's contention with her inherited metaphysic. In death, the soul "That stands for Deity" returns to the spiritual world. The body remains excluded. It is the "Veil" upon this "side" of which the poet remains and which acts as a barrier between herself and God. Spirit and flesh comprise the self, but only the former can partake in the immutable realm.

The dualism of the conception is, in the next stanza, expressed in linguistic terms. The material world is the world of "name" and of "printed" plight. Its life is that of "tender—solemn Alphabet." The poet's accepted fate should be to cross from it into the spiritual world where "name is put away" and alphabet is "smuggled" into eternity. Material language, language as matter, vanishes into the silent, invisible, and bodiless eternal world.

This could be a completion of the self. But the poet sees it as division, as a name torn from self-possession into truncated parts and loyalty. And the poet resists this dissolution. In the last stanzas, she refuses to relinquish any part of herself, calling on her hands to hold that material life against eternity's spiritual banishment of it. Her own material alphabet and "Clay" she declares "Greater than the Gods can show." And she will not let go, for all of heaven's promises, the "Keepsake" of her earthly self.

Dickinson here is caught between spirit and flesh, heaven and earth, silence and speech. They take their place in a structure that defines them as against each other. This structure she can never finally accept. Nor can she accept the structures she attempts to define in their stead. The world of Dickinson's poetry remains pressed between the invisible and the visible, the unspoken and the spoken, in a tension she cannot resolve. She can only raise her voice against a divine world and language that clashes with, but asserts its claim upon her own.

Notes

Introduction

1 *The Poems of Emily Dickinson*, ed. Thomas Johnson (Cambridge, Mass.: Harvard University Press, Belknap Press, 1955), P 1297; hereafter cited in the text as P.

Chapter 1

1 Caesar Blake and Carlton Wells, *The Recognition of Emily Dickinson* (Ann Arbor: University of Michigan Press, 1964), p. 27.

2 Thomas W. Higginson, "Emily Dickinson's Letters," *Atlantic Monthly* 68 (October 1981).

3 Blake and Wells, *The Recognition of Emily Dickinson*, pp. 119, 121.

4 Gertrude Stein, "Poetry and Grammar," in *Lectures in America* (New York: Vintage Books, 1975), p. 209.

5 John Hollander, *Vision and Resonance* (New York: Oxford University Press, 1975), p. 233.

6 Harriet Monroe, "The Single Hound," *Poetry* 5 (December 1914).

7 S. Foster Damon, *Amy Lowell: A Chronicle* (Boston: Houghton Mifflin Co., 1930), p. 295.

8 David Porter, *The Modern Idiom* (Cambridge, Mass.: Harvard University Press, 1981); see discussions, pp. 39–44, 98–102, 120, 75.

9 Brita Lindberg-Seyersted, *The Voice of the Poet* (Upsala, Sweden: Almqvist & Wiksells Boktryckeri AB, 1968), ch. 4.

10 David Porter briefly recounts various interpretations of Dickinson's syntax in *The Art of Emily Dickinson's Early Poetry* (Cambridge, Mass.: Harvard University Press, 1966), pp. 106–07, pp. 134–35.

11 George Whicher, *This Was a Poet* (New York: Charles Scribner's Sons, 1938), p. 234; James Reeves, *Selected Poems of Emily Dickinson* (New York: Macmillan Co., 1959), p. lxvi.

12 Charles Anderson, *Stairway of Surprise* (New York: Holt, Rinehart, & Winston, 1960), p. 67; Thomas Johnson, *Emily Dickinson* (Cambridge, Mass.: Harvard University Press, 1955), p. 93.

13 Sharon Cameron, *Lyric Time* (Baltimore: Johns Hopkins University Press, 1979), p. 1.

14 Ibid., pp. 25, 92, 10.

15 Ibid., p. 46.

16 Kenneth Burke, *The Rhetoric of Religion* (Berkeley: University of California Press, 1970), pp. 142–43, 146.

17 Roland Hagenbuchle, "Precision and Indeterminacy in Dickinson," *ESQ* 70–77, no. 20 (1973–74): 36, 41.

18 Porter, *Modern Idiom*, pp. 120, 54, 138.

19 Cameron, *Lyric Time*, p. 17.

20 Isaac Watts, *Psalms, Hymns and Spiritual Songs* (Boston: James Loring and Lincoln & Edmands, 1832). Hereafter Watts's songs will be cited by their numbers in this arrangement of Watts's work, which corresponds with Edward Dickinson's edition of 1834.

21 Harold Bloom defines the synecdochic implications of Christian typology in an unpublished lecture on the Gospel of John, delivered at the University of Indiana Symposium, 1983.

22 Johnson, *Emily Dickinson*, pp. 84–87.

23 Harvey Gross, *Sound and Form in Modern Poetry* (Ann Arbor: University of Michigan Press, 1964), pp. 3, 18, 19.

24 Clark Griffith, *The Long Shadow* (Princeton: Princeton University Press, 1964), p. 25.

25 Allen Tate, "Emily Dickinson," in *Twentieth Century Views*, ed. R. Sewall (Englewood Cliffs, N.J.: Prentice-Hall, 1963), p. 20.

26 *The Letters of Emily Dickinson*, ed. Thomas Johnson (Cambridge, Mass.: Harvard University Press, Belknap Press, 1958), p. 10; hereafter cited in the text as L.

27 Ralph Waldo Emerson, "Experience," in *Works*, ed. E. W. Emerson (Cambridge, Mass.: Riverside Press, 1904), 3:73.

28 Frank Kermode, *The Sense of an Ending* (New York: Oxford University Press, 1977), pp. 4, 47, 69.

29 Porter, *Modern Idiom*, p. 18.

30 Compare P 599, P 305.

31 Louise Bogan, "A Mystical Poet," in *Emily Dickinson: Three Views* (Amherst, Mass.: Amherst College Press, 1960), p. 28.

32 William R. Sherwood, *Circumference and Circumstance* (New York: Columbia University Press, 1968), p. 138.

33 Robert Weisbuch, *Emily Dickinson's Poetry* (Chicago: University of Chicago Press, 1975), p. 161.

34 Cameron, *Lyric Time*, p. 117.

35 Albert Gelpi, *The Mind of the Poet* (New York: W. W. Norton & Co., 1965), p. 98.

36 Ibid., p. 51. Gelpi is here citing L 968.

37 Compare poems 1411, 1413, 1580, 1646, 1741.

38 Octavio Paz, *Children of the Mire* (Cambridge, Mass.: Harvard University Press, 1974), p. 30.

39 Ibid., pp. 46–50, 31.

40 Friedrich Nietzsche, "The Gay Science," in *The Portable Nietzsche*, ed. and trans. W. Kaufman (Harmondworth, England: Penguin Books, 1968), p. 95.

41 Friedrich Nietzsche, "The Twilight of the Idols," in *The Portable Nietzsche*, pp. 482–83.

42 George Steiner, *Language and Silence* (New York: Atheneum, 1976), p. 64; *Extraterritorial* (New York: Atheneum, 1976), p. 81.

Chapter 2

1 Emily Dickinson, *The Letters of Emily Dickinson*, ed. Thomas Johnson (Cambridge, Mass.: Harvard University Press, Belknap Press, 1958), p. 448.

2 James M. Cox, "Whitman, Twain, and the Civil War," *Sewanee Review* 69, no. 2 (Spring 1961): 185.

3 Henry James, *Notes of a Son and a Brother* (New York: Charles Scribner's Sons, 1914), p. 244.

4 Richard B. Sewall, *The Life of Emily Dickinson* (New York: Farrar, Strauss & Giroux, 1974), p. 536.

5 Thomas Ford, "*Emily Dickinson and the Civil War*," *University Review of Kansas City* 31 (Spring 1965): 199.

6 Karl Keller, *The Only Kangaroo among the Beauty* (Baltimore: John Hopkins University Press, 1979), pp. 110, 104; Porter, *Modern Idiom*, p. 115.

7 Sandra M. Gilbert and Susan Gubar, *The Madwoman in the Attic* (New Haven: Yale University Press, 1979), p. 620.

8 Sewall, *Life*, pp. 33, 54, 117.

9 Jay Leyda, *The Years and Hours of Emily Dickinson* (New Haven: Yale University Press, 1960), 1:394.

10 There are other letters in which the war, although not directly named, may be Dickinson's referent. For example, her remark to Edward Dwight in 1862 that "the World is not the shape it was" (L 246), or that "the World is dead" (L 296).

11 Other poems that apply martial imagery to sunsets or storms are P 152, 594, 666, 1127, 1140, 1415, 1471, 1593.

12 Robert Penn Warren, "Melville's Poems," *Southern Review* 3 (Autumn 1967): 804.

13 Louis Martz, *The Poem of the Mind* (New York: Oxford University Press, 1966), p. 83.

14 *The Viking Portable Walt Whitman*, ed. Mark Van Doren (New York: Viking Press, 1971), pp. 377–78.

15 Martz, *The Poem of the Mind*, pp. 86, 89, 91.

16 James Moorhead, *American Apocalypse* (New Haven: Yale University Press, 1978), p. 43.

17 Ibid., p. 41.

18 Oliver Wendell Holmes, "The Inevitable Trial," in *Glory And Pathos*, ed. Richard Rust (Boston: Holbrook Press, 1970), p. 41.

19 R. L. Stanton, *The Church and the Rebellion* (New York: Derby & Miller, 1864), p. 277.

20 Sacvan Bercovitch, *The Puritan Origins of the American Self* (New Haven: Yale University Press, 1975), p. 89.

21 John Bodo, *The Protestant Clergy and Public Issues, 1812–1848* (Princeton: Princeton University Press, 1954), p. 4.

22 Perry Miller, *The Life of the Mind in America* (New York: Harcourt, Brace & World, 1965), p. 11.

23 Ibid., p. 7.

24 Ernest Lee Tuveson, *Redeemer Nation* (Chicago: University of Chicago Press, 1968), p. 25.

25 H. Richard Niebuhr, *The Kingdom of God in America* (New York: Harper & Row, 1937), p. 51.

26 *Atlantic Monthly* 10 (July 1862).

27 Joyce Sparer Adler, *War in Melville's Imagination* (New York: New York University Press, 1981), p. 134.

28 Emerson, *Works*, 11:160, 516, 514.

29 William Allen Huggard, in *Emerson and the Problem of War and Peace*, University of Iowa Humanistic Studies, vol. 5, no. 5 (1938), fully discusses Emerson's response to the Civil War in terms of his criticism of antebellum America.

30 Ralph Waldo Emerson, *Letters*, ed. R. L. Rusk (New York: Columbia University Press, 1939), 5:252; Emerson, *Works*, 11:342, 354.

31 *Memoranda during the War*, ed. Roy P. Basler (Bloomington: Indiana University Press, 1962), p. 65.

32 *Viking Whitman*, pp. 562–63.

33 Charles I. Glicksberg, ed., *Walt Whitman and the Civil War* (Philadelphia: University of Pennsylvania Press, 1933).

34 Walt Whitman, *The Complete Poems*, ed. Francis Murphy (New York: Penguin Books, 1975), p. 498.

35 Tuveson, *Redeemer Nation*, p. 51.

36 *Harper's Monthly*, October 1858, March 1860, and August 1861.

37 William S. Tyler, *A History of Amherst College 1821–1891* (New York: Frederick Hitchcock, 1895), pp. 267–68, 181.

38 Jay Leyda includes many documents reflecting Amherst involvement with the war in *Years and Hours*, 1:333 and 2:26, 27, 33, 64.

39 Arthur C. Cole, *A Hundred Years of Mount Holyoke College* (New Haven: Yale University Press, 1940), pp. 102, 112. Emily Dickinson's letters of the period present the reactions and uncertainties that the atmosphere of revivals, missions, and fasts caused her. For a full discussion of Dickinson's Holyoke years, see Sewall's *Life* and Sydeny C. Mclean, "Emily Dickinson at Mount Holyoke," *New England Quarterly* 7 (March 1934): 25–42. cf. p. 76 above.

40 Moorhead, *American Apocalypse*, p. 74.

41 Ibid., pp. 49, 70.

42 Merle Curti, "The American Scholar in Three Wars," *Journal of the History of Ideas* 3 (June 1942): 466.

43 Bercovitch, *Puritan Origins*, p. 137.

44 Sydney E. Ahlstrom, *A Religious History of the American People* (New Haven: Yale University Press, 1972), p. 670.

45 Moncure Conway, *Emerson at Home and Abroad* (New York: Haskell House Publishers, 1968), p. 222.

46 Abraham Lincoln, "Meditation on the Divine Will," in *Glory and Pathos*, ed. Rust, pp. 53–54.

47 William Warren Sweet, *The Story of Religion in America* (New York: Harper & Brothers, 1930), p. 449.

48 Sewall, *Life*, pp. 646–47.

49 Daniel Aaron, *The Unwritten War* (New York: Alfred A. Knopf, 1973), p. 356.

50 Rust, ed., *Glory and Pathos*, p. 145.

51 Sacvan Bercovitch, *The American Jeremiad* (Madison: University of Wisconsin Press, 1978), p. 69.

Chapter 3

1 William Fletcher, trans., *The Writings of the Ante-Nicene Fathers*, vol. 7 (Grand Rapids, Mich.: Wm. B. Eerdman, 1951).

2 A. O. Lovejoy, "Milton and the Paradox of the Fortunate Fall," in *Essays in the History of Ideas* (New York: Capricorn Books, 1960), pp. 285–86.

3 John Milton, *Paradise Lost*, ed. Merritt Y. Hughes (New York: Odyssey Press, Bobbs-Merrill Co., 1957), p. 465.

4 John Hick, *Evil and the God of Love* (Norfolk, England: Collins, Fontana Library, 1968), p. 182.

5 George M. Fredrickson, *The Inner Civil War* (New York: Harper & Row, 1965), pp. 79–81.

6 Tuveson, *Redeemer Nation*, p. 195.

7 R. L. Stanton, *The Church and the Rebellion* (New York: Derby & Miller, 1864), pp. 277, 281.

8 Lawrence Sargent Hall, *Hawthorne, Critic of Society* (Gloucester, Mass.: Peter Smith, 1966), p. 151.

9 Ralph Waldo Emerson, *Journals*, ed. E. W. Emerson (Boston: Houghton Mifflin Co., 1913), 9:245–46.

10 Nathaniel Hawthorne, "Chiefly about War-Matters," *Atlantic Monthly* 10 (July 1862).

11 Daniel Aaron, *The Unwritten War* (New York: Alfred A. Knopf, 1973), p. 62.

12 Edmund Wilson, *Patriotic Gore* (New York: Oxford University Press, 1962), p. 98.

13 Moorhead, *American Apocalypse*, p. 176.

14 Aaron, *Unwritten War*, p. 351.

15 Fredrickson, *Inner Civil War*, p. 96.

16 Whitman, *Complete Poems*, p. 457.

17 Bercovitch, *American Jeremiad*, pp. 51–52.

18 Jonathan Edwards, *The Works of President Edwards*, Worcester ed. (New York: Leavitt & Allen, 1851), 3:291, 458, 481, 417.

19 Bercovitch, *American Jeremiad,* pp. 101, 174.

20 Hick, *Evil and the God of Love,* p. 173.

21 Theodore Minnema, "Calvin's Interpretation of Human Suffering," in *Exploring the Heritage of John Calvin,* ed. D. Holwerda (Grand Rapids, Mich.: Baker Book House, 1976), p. 154.

22 Ronald S. Wallace, *Calvin's Doctrine of the Christian Life* (Grand Rapids, Mich.: Wm. B. Eerdman, 1959), pp. 198, 263.

23 Hick, *Evil and the God of Love,* p. 88.

24 Edward A. Dowey, *The Knowledge of God in Calvin's Theology* (New York: Columbia University Press, 1952), p. 213.

25 Edwards, *Works,* 2:162–63.

26 Ibid., 2:462, 465.

27 Thomas Le Duc, *Piety and Intellect at Amherst College* (New York: Arno Press and the *New York Times,* 1969), p. 3.

28 John Marsh, *An Epitome of General Ecclesiastical History* (New York: Tilden & Co., 1854), p. 319.

29 Michael Wigglesworth, *The Day of Doom,* ed. K. B. Murdock (New York: Russel & Russel, 1966), verses 67, 197.

30 Sewall, *Life,* p. 360; see also Mclean, "Emily Dickinson at Mount Holyoke," pp. 25–42.

31 Edwards, *Works,* 4:423.

32 F. D. Huntington, *Christian Believing and Living* (Boston: Crosby, Nichols & Co., 1860), p. 84.

33 Ibid., p. 91.

34 John Calvin, *Institutes of the Christian Religion,* trans. John Allen (Philadelphia: Presbyterian Board of Christian Education, 1928), Book 1, p. 47; Book 3, p. 630.

35 Minnema, "Calvin's Interpretation of Human Suffering," p. 146.

36 Wallace, *Calvin's Doctrine,* pp. 43–44, 314.

37 Huntington, *Christian Believing,* pp. 276, 344, 340.

38 Sewall, *Life,* 2:688–94. Jack Capps similarly accepts the *Imitation* as a model for Dickinson without ironies in *Emily Dickinson's Reading* (Cambridge, Mass.: Harvard University Press, 1966), p. 61.

39 Richard Wilbur, "Sumptuous Destitution," in *Emily Dickinson, Three Views,* pp. 40–41.

40 Margaret Homans, *Women Writers and Poetic Identity* (Princeton: Princeton University Press, 1980), pp. 176–77.

41 Henry W. Wells, *Introduction to Emily Dickinson* (Chicago: Packard & Co., 1947), p. 144.

42 Porter, *Modern Idiom,* p. 99.

43 Keller, *Only Kangaroo,* p. 5.

44 Le Duc, *Piety and Intellect,* pp. 2–3.

45 Bercovitch, *American Jeremiad,* p. 173.

46 Joseph Haroutunian, *Piety vs. Moralism: The Passing of New England Theology* (Hamden, Conn.: Anchor Books, 1964), pp. 179–82.

47 Robert C. Albrecht, "The Theological Response of the Transcendentalists to the Civil War," *New England Quarterly* 38 (March 1965): 21.

48 F. O. Mathiessen, *American Renaissance* (New York: Oxford University Press, 1968), p. 179.

49 Herman Melville, "Hawthorne and His Mosses, *The Apple-Tree Table* (New York: Greenwood Press, 1922), pp. 62–63.

50 Nathaniel Hawthorne, *The Marble Faun* (New York: Signet Classic, New American Library, 1961), p. 329.

51 Albrecht, "Theological Response," p. 32.

52 Mathiessen, *American Renaissance*, p. 185.

53 Emerson, *Works*, 2:102, 126; 6:35.

54 Keller, *Only Kangaroo*, pp. 87, 90.

55 Emerson, *Works*, 12:405, 414.

56 R. W. Emerson, *Works*, ed. E. W. Emerson (Boston: Houghton Mifflin Co., 1913), 3:49.

57 Harold Bloom, *The Ringers in the Tower* (Chicago: University of Chicago Press, 1971), p. 226.

58 Clark Griffith, *The Long Shadow* (Princeton: Princeton University Press, 1964), p. 232. See also Homans, *Women Writers*, p. 176.

59 Bruce Catton, *America Goes to War* (Middletown, Conn.: Wesleyan University Press, 1958), ch. 3.

60 Charles Anderson, *Stairway of Surprise* (New York: Holt, Rinehart, & Winston, 1960), p. 174.

61 Johnson, *Emily Dickinson*, p. 139.

62 Porter, *Modern Idiom*, pp. 209, 216.

63 John Cody, *After Great Pain* (Cambridge, Mass.: Harvard University Press, Belknap Press, 1971), p. 332.

64 Cameron, *Lyric Time*, p. 71.

65 Ibid., p. 66.

66 Lovejoy, "Milton and the Paradox of the Fortunate Fall," in *Essays*, p. 279.

Chapter 4

1 See, for example, Ruth Flanders Mcnaughton, *The Imagery of Emily Dickinson* (New York: Folcraft Library Editions, 1973); Mabel Loomis Todd and Thomas W. Higginson, eds., *Favorite Poems of Emily Dickinson* (New York: Avenel Books, 1978); Louis Unterermeyer, ed., *Poems of Emily Dickinson* (New York: Heritage Press, 1952).

2 T. S. Eliot, "Baudelaire," in *Selected Essays* (New York: Harcourt, Brace & World, 1964), p. 373.

3 Donald Thackrey, "The Communication of the Word," in *Emily Dickinson: Twentieth Century Views*, ed. R. Sewall (Englewood Cliffs, N.J.: Prentice Hall, 1963), p. 51.

4 Porter, *Modern Idiom*, pp. 106, 238.

5 Northrop Frye, *Secular Scripture*, Charles Eliot Norton lectures (Cambridge, Mass.: Harvard University Press, 1976), p. 47.

6 Ralph Barton Perry, *Puritanism and Democracy* (New York: Vanguard Press, 1944), p. 316.
7 Marvin Meyers, *The Jacksonian Persuasion* (Stanford: Calif.: Stanford University Press, 1957), pp. 181, 167.
8 Emerson, *Works*, 2:94.
9 Perry Miller, "The Marrow of Puritan Divinity," *Publications of the Colonial Society of Massachusetts* 32 (1933–37): 260–62.
10 Nietzsche, "Twilight of the Idols," in *The Portable Nietzsche*, pp. 484–85.
11 Friedrich Nietzsche, *The Will to Power*, ed. Walter Kaufman (New York: Vintage Books, 1967), #8, p. 11.
12 Friedrich Nietzsche, "The Antichrist," in *The Portable Nietzsche*, pp. 575, 582.
13 Ibid., p. 581.
14 Nietzsche, *Will to Power*, #351, p. 193.
15 Poem 1373 as treated here is a variant version to that adopted by Johnson in the *Complete Poems*.
16 *The Letters of Emily Dickinson*, ed. Thomas Johnson (Cambridge, Mass.: Harvard University Press, Belknap Press, 1958), p. 20; prose fragments from this edition hereafter cited in text as PF.
17 Nietzsche, *Will to Power*, #196, p. 116.
18 Griffith, *Long Shadow*, p. 167.
19 David Porter, in *The Art of Emily Dickinson's Early Poetry* (Cambridge, Mass.: Harvard University Press, 1966), p. 174, suggests that only if the divine were subject to despair could it respond.
20 Anderson, *Stairway of Surprise*, pp. 29–30.
21 Herman Melville, *Pierre* (New York: Signet Classic, New American Library, 1964), p. 247.
22 Emerson, *Works*, 6:207; 3:17, 15; 2:292.
23 Ibid., 2:272, 273, 302.
24 Ibid., 6:254; 8:333.
25 Homans, *Women Writers*, p. 183.
26 Emerson, *Works*, 4:185–86. At the end of his essay on Montaigne, Emerson is in fact quoting Ellery Channing's "If my bark sink / 'Tis to another sea."
27 Anderson cites Sir Thomas Browne's *Religio Medici* as Dickinson's source for this definition (*Stairway of Surprise*, p. 55), and Gelpi cites Emerson in *Mind of the Poet*, p. 122. The image is not uncommon; Isaac Watts includes an image similar to it in a hymn to God as "The Circle where my passions move / And Centre of my Soul" (170).
28 Anderson, *Stairway*, p. 55.
29 Gelpi, *Mind of the Poet*, pp. 122–23.
30 Emerson, *Works*, 2:60, 70. For a complete discussion of synecdoche and its implications, see chapter I.
31 Griffith, in *The Long Shadow*, pp. 211–13, discusses the ironies of Dickinson's poems of the imperial self, although in a different context.
32 Griffith, *The Long Shadow*, p. 212.

33 Anderson, *Stairway*, p. 171.

34 Emerson, *Works*, 2:317–18.

35 Compare, for example, P 695.

Chapter 5

1 Ronald S. Wallace, *Calvin's Doctrine of the Word and Sacrament* (Grand Rapids, Mich.: William B. Eerdman's Publishing Co., 1957), pp. 98–99.

2 Ursula Brumm, *American Thought and Religious Typology* (New Brunswick, N.J.: Rutgers University Press, 1970), p. 32.

3 Emory Elliott, "From Father to Son: The Evolution of Typology in Puritan New England," in *Literary Uses of Typology*, ed. E. Miner (Princeton: Princeton University Press, 1977), pp. 204–05.

4 Keller, *Only Kangaroo*, p. 123.

5 Brumm, *American Thought*, pp. 22, 30.

6 Erich Auerbach, *Mimesis* (Princeton: Princeton University Press, 1953), p. 74.

7 Erich Auerbach, "Figura," in *Scenes from the Drama of European Literature* (New York: Meridian Books, 1959), p. 53.

8 Ibid., p. 60.

9 John Calvin, *Commentary on the Gospel according to John* (Grand Rapids, Mich.: William B. Eerdman's Publishing Co., 1949), John 9:5, 1:369.

10 Compare Whitman's "Chanting the Square Deific" where "dear brothers and sisters" are similarly named.

11 J. N. Sanders and B. A. Martin, *A Commentary on the Gospel according to St. John* (New York: Harper & Row, 1968), p. 19.

12 Edwin Hatch, *The Influence of Greek Ideas and Usages upon the Christian Church*, Hibbert lectures, 1888 (London: Williams & Norgate, 1891), pp. 178–79.

13 Rudolph Bultmann, *The Gospel of John, a Commentary* (Oxford: Basil Blackwell, 1971), pp. 20–21.

14 Hatch, *Influence*, p. 177.

15 C. H. Dodd, "The Background of the Fourth Gospel," *John Rylands Library* (Manchester) 19, no. 1 (January 1935): 342.

16 Ibid., p. 343.

17 Bultmann, *Commentary*, pp. 21, 35.

18 Augustine, "On the Trinity," in *Basic Writings of Saint Augustine*, ed. Whitney J. Oates (New York: Random House, 1948), vol. I, bk. XV, chs. xi, viii, xiv, xi.

19 Ibid., bk. XV, ch. xvi.

20 Martin Luther, "Sermons on the Gospel of St. John, chapters 1–4," in *Martin Luther's Works*, ed. Jaroslav Pelikan (St. Louis: Concordia Publishing House, 1957), 22:9.

21 Wallace, *Calvin's Doctrine of the Word*, p. 12.

22 Ibid.

23 Burke, *Rhetoric of Religion*, pp. 13, 16–17.

24 Hatch, *Influence*, p. 262.

25 Anderson, *Stairway of Surprise*, p. 94.
26 Weisbuch, *Emily Dickinson's Poetry*, pp. 79, 175.
27 Cameron, *Lyric Time*, pp. 89–90.
28 Jack Capps, in *Emily Dickinson's Reading* (Cambridge, Mass.: Harvard University Press, 1966), p. 154, cites Daniel 8:16 as the poem's reference.
29 See, for example, "Title Divine is Mine" (P 1072); "Only a Shrine, but Mine" (P 918); "Through the Straight Pass" (P 792).
30 *The Wohunge of Ure Lauerd*, ed. W. Meredith Thompson, Early English Text Society, no. 241 (London: Oxford University Press, 1955), p. 36.
31 See discussion in chapter I concerning Dickinson's interest in Thomas a Kempis's *The Imitation of Christ*.
32 Cameron, *Lyric Time*, p. 40.
33 Augustine, *On the Trinity*, bk. XV, ch. xi; bk. IX, ch. viii; bk. XV, ch. xi.
34 Jacques Derrida, *Of Grammatology*, trans. G. C. Spivak (Baltimore; Johns Hopkins University Press, 1976), p. 13.
35 See Dickinson's correspondence in *Letters* with Helen Hunt Jackson on the question of publication, and Whicher, *This Was a Poet*, pp. 122 ff., for a discussion of Helen Hunt Jackson's persistent urging of Dickinson to publish her poems.
36 See chapter 4 for a discussion of the theological implications of Dickinson's contractual language.
37 Emerson, *Works*, 3:3; 2:276, 273.

Selected Bibliography

Aaron, Daniel. *The Unwritten War.* New York: Alfred A. Knopf, 1973.

Adler, Joyce Sparer. *War in Melville's Imagination.* New York: New York University Press, 1981.

Ahlstrom, Sydney E. *A Religious History of the American People.* New Haven: Yale University Press, 1972.

Albrecht, Robert C. "The Theological Response of the Transcendentalists to the Civil War." *New England Quarterly* 38 (March 1965).

Anderson, Charles. *Stairway of Surprise.* New York: Holt, Rinehart, & Winston, 1960.

Auerbach, Erich. "Figura." In *Scenes from the Drama of European Literature.* New York: Meridian Books, 1959.

———. *Mimesis.* Princeton: Princeton University Press, 1953.

Bercovitch, Sacvan. *The American Jeremiad.* Madison: University of Wisconsin Press, 1978.

———. *The Puritan Origins of the American Self.* New Haven: Yale University Press, 1975.

Blake, Caesar, and Wells, Carlton. *The Recognition of Emily Dickinson.* Ann Arbor: University of Michigan Press, 1964.

Bloom, Harold. "The Gospel of John." Unpublished lecture delivered at Conference on "The Sacred Text," Indiana University, Bloomington, 1982.

———. *The Ringers in the Tower.* Chicago: University of Chicago Press, 1971.

Bodo, John. *The Protestant Clergy and Public Issues, 1812–1848.* Princeton: Princeton University Press, 1954.

Bogan, Louise. "A Mystical Poet." In *Emily Dickinson: Three Views.* Amherst: Amherst College Press, 1960.

Brumm, Ursula. *American Thought and Religious Typology.* New Brunswick, N.J.: Rutgers University Press, 1970.

Bultmann, Rudolph. *The Gospel of John, a Commentary.* Oxford: Basil Blackwell, 1971.

Burke, Kenneth. *The Rhetoric of Religion.* Berkeley: University of California Press, 1970.

Calvin, John. *Commentary on the Gospel according to John.* Vol. 1. Grand Rapids, Mich.: William B. Eerdman's Publishing Co., 1949.

―――. *Institutes of the Christian Religion.* Translated by John Allen. Philadelphia: Presbyterian Board of Christian Education, 1928.

Cameron, Sharon. *Lyric Time.* Baltimore: Johns Hopkins University Press, 1979.

Capps, Jack. *Emily Dickinson's Reading.* Cambridge, Mass.: Harvard University Press, 1966.

Catton, Bruce. *America Goes to War.* Middletown, Conn.: Wesleyan University Press, 1958.

Cody, John. *After Great Pain.* Cambridge, Mass.: Harvard University Press, Belknap Press, 1971.

Cole, Arthur C. *A Hundred Years of Mount Holyoke College.* New Haven: Yale University Press, 1940.

Conway, Moncure. *Emerson at Home and Abroad.* New York: Haskell House Publishers, 1968.

Cox, James M. "Whitman, Twain, and the Civil War." *Sewanee Review* 69, no. 2 (Spring 1961).

Curti, Merle. "The American Scholar in Three Wars." *Journal of the History of Ideas* 3 (June 1942).

Damon, S. Foster. *Amy Lowell: A Chronicle.* Boston: Houghton Mifflin Co., 1930.

Derrida, Jacques. *Of Grammatology.* Translated by G. C. Spivak. Baltimore: Johns Hopkins University Press, 1976.

Dodd, C. H. "The Background of the Fourth Gospel." *John Rylands Library* (Manchester) 19, no. 1 (January 1935).

Dowey, Edward A. *The Knowledge of God in Calvin's Theology.* New York: Columbia University Press, 1952.

Edwards, Jonathan. *The Works of President Edwards,* Worcester ed. New York: Leavitt & Allen, 1851.

Eliot, T. S. "Baudelaire." In *Selected Essays.* New York: Harcourt, Brace & World, 1964.

Elliott, Emory. "From Father to Son: The Evolution of Typology in Puritan New England." In *Literary Uses of Typology.* Edited by E. Miner. Princeton: Princeton University Press, 1977.

Emerson, Ralph Waldo. *The Journals of R. W. Emerson.* Edited by E. W. Emerson. Boston: Houghton Mifflin Co., 1913.

―――. *The Letters of R. W. Emerson.* Edited by R. L. Rusk. New York: Columbia University Press, 1939.

————. *The Works of R. W. Emerson.* Edited by E. W. Emerson. Cambridge, Mass.: Riverside Press, 1904.

Fletcher, William, trans. *The Writings of the Ante-Nicene Fathers.* Vol. 7. Grand Rapids, Mich.: Wm. B. Eerdman, 1951.

Ford, Thomas. "Emily Dickinson and the Civil War." *University Review of Kansas City* 31 (Spring 1965).

Fredrickson, George M. *The Inner Civil War.* New York: Harper & Row, 1965.

Frye, Northrop. *Secular Scripture.* Charles Eliot Norton lectures. Cambridge, Mass.: Harvard University Press, 1976.

Gelpi, Albert. *The Mind of the Poet.* New York: W. W. Norton & Co., 1965.

Gilbert, Sandra M., and Gubar, Susan. *The Madwoman in the Attic.* New Haven: Yale University Press, 1979.

Glicksberg, Charles I., ed. *Walt Whitman and the Civil War.* Philadelphia: University of Pennsylvania Press, 1933.

Griffith, Clark. *The Long Shadow.* Princeton: Princeton University Press, 1964.

Gross, Harvey. *Sound and Form in Modern Poetry.* Ann Arbor: University of Michigan Press, 1964.

Hagenbuchle, Roland. "Precision and Indeterminacy in Dickinson." *ESQ* 70–77, no. 20 (1973–74).

Hall, Lawrence Sargent. *Hawthorne, Critic of Society.* Gloucester, Mass.: Peter Smith, 1966.

Haroutinian, Joseph. *Piety vs. Moralism: The Passing of New England Theology.* Hamden, Conn.: Anchor Books, 1964.

Hatch, Edwin. *The Influence of Greek Ideas and Usages upon the Christian Church.* Hibbert lectures, 1888. London: Williams & Norgate, 1891.

Hawthorne, Nathaniel. "Chiefly about War-Matters." *Atlantic Monthly* 10 (July 1862).

————. *The Marble Faun.* Indianapolis: Bobbs-Merrill, 1971.

————. *Our Old Home.* New York: T. Y. Crowell and Co., 1906.

Hick, John. *Evil and the God of Love.* Norfolk, England: Collins, Fontana Library, 1968.

Higginson, Thomas Wentworth. "Emily Dickinson's Letters." *Atlantic Monthly* 68 (October 1981).

Hollander, John. *Vision and Resonance.* New York: Oxford University Press, 1975.

Holmes, Oliver Wendell. "The Inevitable Trial." In *Glory and Pathos.* Edited by Richard Rust. Boston: Holbrook Press, 1970.

Homans, Margaret. *Women Writers and Poetic Identity.* Princeton: Princeton University Press, 1980.

Huggard, William Allen. "Emerson and the Problem of War and Peace." *University of Iowa Studies*, no. 353 (April 1938).

Huntington, F. D. *Christian Believing and Living*. Boston: Crosby, Nichols & Co., 1860.

James, Henry. *Notes of a Son and a Brother*. New York: Charles Scribner's Sons, 1914.

Johnson, Thomas. *Emily Dickinson*. Cambridge, Mass.: Harvard University Press, 1955.

Keller, Karl. *The Only Kangaroo among the Beauty*. Baltimore: John Hopkins University Press, 1979.

Kermode, Frank. *The Sense of an Ending*. New York: Oxford University Press, 1977.

Le Duc, Thomas. *Piety and Intellect at Amherst College*. New York: Arno Press and the *New York Times*, 1969.

Leyda, Jay. *The Years and Hours of Emily Dickinson*. New Haven: Yale University Press, 1960.

Lincoln, Abraham. "Meditation on the Divine Will." In *Glory and Pathos*. Edited by Richard Rust. Boston: Holbrook Press, 1970.

Lindberg-Seyersted, Brita. *The Voice of the Poet*. Upsala, Sweden: Almqvist & Wiksells Boktryckeri AB, 1968.

Lovejoy, A. O. "Milton and the Paradox of the Fortunate Fall." In *Essays in the History of Ideas*. New York: Capricorn Books, 1960.

Luther, Martin. "Sermons on the Gospel of St. John, chapters 1–4." In *Martin Luther's Works*. Edited by J. Pelikan. Vol. 22. St. Louis: Concordia Publishing House, 1957.

Marsh, John. *An Epitome of General Ecclesiastical History*. New York: Tilden & Co., 1854.

Martz, Louis. *The Poem of the Mind*. New York: Oxford University Press, 1966.

Mathiessen, F. O. *American Renaissance*. New York: Oxford University Press, 1968.

Mclean, Sydeny C. "Emily Dickinson at Mount Holyoke." *New England Quarterly* 7 (March 1934).

Mcnaughton, Ruth Flanders. *The Imagery of Emily Dickinson*. New York: Folcraft Library Editions, 1973.

Melville, Herman. *Battle-Pieces*. New York: Harper & Brothers, 1866.

———. "Hawthorne and His Mosses." In *The Apple Tree Table*. New York: Greenwood Press, 1922.

———. *Pierre*. New York: Signet Classic, New American Library, 1964.

Meyers, Marvin. *The Jacksonian Persuasion*. Stanford, Calif.: Stanford University Press, 1944.

Miller, Perry. *The Life of the Mind in America*. New York: Harcourt, Brace & World, 1965.

———. "The Marrow of Puritan Divinity." *Publications of the Colonial Society of Massachusetts* 32 (1933–37).

Milton, John. *Complete Poems and Major Prose*. Edited by M. Hughes. New York: Bobbs-Merrill Co., 1957.

Minnema, Theodore. "Calvin's Interpretation of Human Suffering." In *Exploring the Heritage of John Calvin*. Edited by D. Holwerda. Grand Rapids, Mich.: Baker Book House, 1976.

Monroe, Harriet. "The Single Hound." *Poetry* 5 (December 1914).

Moorhead, James. *American Apocalypse*. New Haven: Yale University Press, 1978.

Niebuhr, Richard H. *The Kingdom of God in America*. New York: Harper & Row, 1937.

Nietzsche, Friedrich. "The Anti-Christ." In *The Portable Nietzsche*. Edited and translated by Walter Kaufman. Harmondworth, England: Penguin Books, 1976.

———. "The Gay Science." In *The Portable Nietzsche*. Edited and translated by Walter Kaufman. Harmondworth, England: Penguin Books, 1968.

———. "The Twilight of the Idols." In *The Portable Nietzsche*. Edited and translated by Walter Kaufman. Harmondworth, England: Penguin Books, 1968.

———. *The Will to Power*. Edited by Walter Kaufman. New York: Vintage Books, 1967.

Paz, Octavio. *Children of the Mire*. Cambridge, Mass.: Harvard University Press, 1974.

Perry, Ralph Barton. *Puritanism and Democracy*. New York: Vanguard Press, 1944.

Porter, David. *The Art of Emily Dickinson's Early Poetry*. Cambridge, Mass.: Harvard University Press, 1966.

———. *The Modern Idiom*. Cambridge, Mass.: Harvard University Press, 1981.

Reeves, James. *Selected Poems of Emily Dickinson*. New York: Macmillan Co., 1959.

Rust, Richard, ed. *Glory and Pathos*. Boston: Holbrook Press, 1970.

Saint Augustine. "On the Trinity." In *Basic Writings of Saint Augustine*. Edited by Whitney J. Oates. New York: Random House, 1948.

Sewall, Richard B. *The Life of Emily Dickinson*. New York: Farrar, Strauss & Giroux, 1974.

Sherwood, William R. *Circumference and Circumstance*. New York: Columbia University Press, 1968.

Stanton, R. L. *The Church and the Rebellion*. New York: Derby & Miller, 1864.

Stein, Gertrude. "Poetry and Grammar." In *Lectures in America*. New York: Vintage Books, 1975.

Steiner, George. *Extraterritorial*. New York: Atheneum, 1976.

―――. *Language and Silence*. New York: Atheneum, 1976.

Sweet, William Warren. *The Story of Religion in America*. New York: Harper & Brothers, 1930.

Tate, Allen. "Emily Dickinson." In *Emily Dickinson: Twentieth Century Views*. Edited by R. Sewall. Englewood Cliffs, N.J.: Prentice-Hall, 1963.

Thackrey, Donald. "The Communication of the Word." In *Emily Dickinson: Twentieth Century Views*. Edited by R. Sewall. Englewood Cliffs, N.J.: Prentice-Hall, 1963.

Thomas a Kempis, *Of the Imitation of Christ*. London: Rovington's, 1876.

Todd, Mabel Loomis, and Higginson, Thomas W., eds. *Favorite Poems of Emily Dickinson*. New York: Avenel Books, 1978.

Tuveson, Ernest Lee. *Redeemer Nation*. Chicago: University of Chicago Press, 1968.

Tyler, William S. *A History of Amherst College, 1821–1891*. New York: Frederick Hitchcock, 1895.

Untermeyer, Louis, ed. *Poems of Emily Dickinson*. New York: Heritage Press, 1952.

Wallace, Ronald. *Calvin's Doctrine of the Christian Life*. Grand Rapids, Mich.: William B. Eerdman, 1959.

―――. *Calvin's Doctrine of the Word and Sacrament*. Grand Rapids, Mich.: William B. Eerdman's Publishing Co., 1957.

Warren, Robert Penn. "Melville's Poems." *Southern Review* 3 (Autumn 1967).

Watts, Isaac. *Psalms, Hymns, and Spiritual Songs*. Boston: James Loring and Lincoln & Edmands, 1832.

Weisbuch, Robert. *Emily Dickinson's Poetry*. Chicago: University of Chicago Press, 1975.

Wells, Henry W. *Introduction to Emily Dickinson*. Chicago: Packard & Co., 1947.

Whicher, George. *This Was a Poet*. New York: Charles Scribner's Sons, 1938.

Whitman, Walt. *The Complete Poems*. Edited by Francis Murphy. New York: Penguin Books, 1975.

―――. *The Viking Portable Walt Whitman*. Edited by Mark Van Doren. New York: Viking Press, 1971.

————. *Memoranda during the War*. Edited by Roy P. Basler. Bloomington: Indiana University Press, 1962.

Wigglesworth, Michael. *The Day of Doom*. Edited by Kenneth B. Murdock. New York: Russel & Russel, 1966.

Wilbur, Richard. "Sumptuous Destitution." In *Emily Dickinson: Three Views*. Amherst: Amherst College Press, 1960.

Wilson, Edmund. *Patriotic Gore*. New York: Oxford University Press, 1962.

The Wohunge of Ure Lauerd. Edited by W. Meredith Thompson. Early English Text Society, no. 241. London: Oxford University Press, 1955.

Index of Poems Discussed

The Index of Poems Discussed includes those poems that are quoted at length and fully treated. Poems cited in the course of my discussion are excluded. P designates *The Poems of Emily Dickinson*, published by Harvard University Press.

191

General Index

Amherst: war dead, 33, 39, 43, 60, 61–62; and Dickinson family, 34–35; and war, 52–54, 60; and Calvinism, 73–77, 88–89

Augustine, Saint: and syntax, 5–6; and synecdoche, 10, 126; on evil, 73–74; and Logos, 146–48, 149, 165–66

Battle Hymn of the Republic, The, 46, 51

Bible, references to: Old Testament, 26, 94, 139, 182; New Testament, 59, 61–62, 136, 143, 150, 151, 164, 168. *See also* Typology

Blasphemy: defined, xiv, xix–xx, 99–100, 102; and language, 116, 117–18, 122–23, 134–35; and prayer, 118, 121, 134–35

Bowles, Samuel, 35, 36, 136, 160

Brown, John, 69–70

Calvin, John, 73–74, 76, 78–79, 138, 142, 148

Calvinism, 31, 127; and American national identity, 46–48, 75–79; and evil, 71–79; in Amherst, 73–77, 88–89; and secularization, 88–90; and covenant theology, 107. *See also* Metaphysical critique; Typology

Causality, xv, 9–10, 18–19, 30

Circumference, 95, 97, 125–27, 130–31

Covenant theology, 105–08, 167

Death, 27, 29; and immortality, 5–6, 42, 43–44, 67, 72, 100–01, 109–10, 116–17, 139; and war, 37, 40–45, 51, 56, 72, 77; and silence, 163–64. *See also* Theodicy

Derrida, Jacques, 165

Design, 4, 38, 44, 137–38

Dickinson, Austin, 34, 106

Dickinson, Edward, 34–35, 53

Dickinson, Emily: and reclusion, xiii–xiv, xvii–xviii, 31, 32–35, 36, 127–30, 160, 167; and religious conflict: xiv, 25–26, 31, 32, 49, 101, 102–03, 109, 113, 134; schooling of, 54, 75, 76, 176; prose fragments of, 116, 147. *See also* Amherst

Dickinson's letters: and loss, 17, 119, 161; and religion, 26, 76, 101, 106, 109, 113, 115, 116, 118, 124, 126, 134, 139, 141, 163; and war, 35–37, 39, 42, 56–57, 61, 83, 175; and theodicy, 44–45, 68, 136; and death, 103, 168; and language, 126, 136, 163

Dickinson, Susan Gilbert, 36, 80

Dualism, 124–25, 148, 150, 164–66, 167–71

Edwards, Jonathan, 88; and evil, 73–75; and Amherst, 75–78

Emerson, Ralph Waldo, xvi, 18, 106, 133, 169; and war, 33, 49–50, 62, 69; and Transcendentalism, 90, 124–25;